12 Weeks
of Winter
and Beyond

Uncharted Territory
After Sudden Death

Sandy McBay

 FriesenPress

Suite 300 - 990 Fort St
Victoria, BC, Canada, V8V 3K2
www.friesenpress.com

Copyright © 2015 by Sandy McBay
First Edition — 2015

Floyd Elzinga, Artist

ISBN
978-1-4602-6486-7 (Hardcover)
978-1-4602-6487-4 (Paperback)
978-1-4602-6488-1 (eBook)

1. Religion, Faith

Distributed to the trade by The Ingram Book Company

Table of Contents

Introduction

It is possible that the number of books written about grief in the past forty years could only be surpassed by the number of diet/get thin quick manuals. While a bit 'tongue in cheek' this sentiment may well define the initial reaction to this book: *Another book on grieving?*

I might have well asked that same question three years ago; having been immersed in the topic for a good part of my life (my work in palliative care and bereavement support), I have seen and read a lot of them, albeit I am aware that I've only scratched the surface. Could it be that the mantra of "the reactions of grief are as unique and equal in number to the deaths that have spanned a lifetime" explains the proliference of said books?

However, having had to come to terms with the loss of my husband, I decided to write my own story, and one that would be designed to help others who were overwhelmed with grief. Having started writing, I sent a colleague of mine, Harry van Bommel, the premise of my story in return for his personal thoughts and literary feedback. Harry is a speaker and writer of many palliative resource books and has been a good and consistent friend to me.

I had prefaced the message with the comment: "I am not sure where this is going beyond its therapeutic value, but I also wonder if it might be helpful to someone else?"

Harry's response was most gracious and he encouraged me to "keep writing". If my story is enough to help just one person on the planet find a way to give voice to their grief, I am privileged. And, I pray it gives some kind of meaning to my husband's life, who was taken from us far too soon.

Theories on bereavement support continue to evolve. Kubler Ross's five stages have been receiving less than glowing reviews the past couple of decades, but we must respect her ability to get the conversation started. William Worden, Therese Rando, Alan Wolfelt, Kenneth Doka and a host of others have expanded our understanding of what it is to grieve. And yet the books continue to show up in the self-help sections of our favourite book stores.

As we continue to evolve from our Creator breathed origin, we learn more about the human condition. Over the centuries, our responses to death have wavered between accepting this most important final task of life as normal; and sterilizing it by pushing it out of the family home into the capable hands of the professionals. Some would ask, "At what expense?"

I have come to respect the fact that we each have a story to tell on the subject of death, and we can learn a great deal from one another in that respect. While *we need to respect the great works from our more academic writers on grief, we have much to learn from each other's stories. Because I have learned academically and personally from the experiences of many as well as my own, I submit that there are still more important things to tell and learn. Twelve Weeks of Winter and Beyond* is my own personal experience, a story I have written over a period of two years since my husband Rick died. While there is nothing new under the sun, there are new people dying every second and new loved ones left behind to navigate the fog while reaching out for some semblance of normal. And in honour of Rick, this book has been written to fulfil his wish that I write, something that he encouraged me to do throughout our years of marriage.

As well, words have always been a treasure to me and I frustrate easily when they do not come forth to match the thoughts of the joy and sorrow in my heart. Punctuation has never been my strength. From the stunning movie "Wit" which I used in my palliative teaching, comes a most wonderful line. Professor Vivian Bearing, who in her late forties was diagnosed with fourth stage ovarian cancer, "there is no fifth stage" stated Vivian, cited a memory from when she was being counselled as a student by her 17th Century English literature mentor, Professor Ashford. In Vivian's essay on the Poet John Dunne, Professor Ashford accused Vivian of 'hysterical punctuation', inserting exclamation marks and commas where none should have been used. Ashford firmly yet gently reminded Vivian that words bore out their own meaning and most of the time, did not require punctuation, underlining or capitals to help the reader grasp those meanings. *Guilty as charged.* "Sometimes just a comma, "a pause" is all that separates life and death.

In an effort to give balance to this project, others have been invited to tell their stories. Sadly, they have had to restrict themselves quantitatively to allow for several submissions. I thank them for honouring my request and allowing themselves to look back, at the risk perhaps of reliving some painful memories. But I believe it is the telling of the story that continues to release the pain, allowing us to move forward. And it is the telling of the story that gives meaning to those who died. For those who read these pages, I hope you find solace, which will in turn offer greater clarity and the strength to deal with the loss of your loved ones.

Chapter 1

Seasons, Pathways and Medicine Wheels

Antonio Vivaldi created glorious music in his short, sixty-three years of life. He was apparently a redhead, which to some may explain the wonder of his *Four Seasons*. I confess I appreciate more the spring and summer months, while there are times when my mood dictates the haunting and even harsher notes from the fall and winter seasons.

On December 11, 2010, my husband Rick, died suddenly and most unexpectedly. To help me begin to make sense of my new life I decided to write a book, which I called *Twelve Weeks of Winter*. Over the years many people – including my husband – have encouraged me to write. With Rick's death, the time had come for me to assign the words most suited to my reality and the feelings which accompany them.

My husband, John Richard McBay, died from an aortic dissection at approximately 9:50 pm on the aforementioned December 11, 2010. For those who have embraced the death of a loved one, they will understand the intensity of date and time and the need to have them perhaps forever emblazed in their memory. Somehow, it adds to the meaning of the unwelcomeness.

Twelve Weeks of Winter has taken on several different definitions since I began writing it, and as such, has evolved to 'beyond' being added to the title. Initially, my desire to chronicle my experience and the immense felt support over the first twelve weeks, or as some have described it, *the first 100 days*, was the impetus behind my story. But, as I "explored and was curious" as a wise counsellor suggested, about where I would be two years later, I wondered. And, as I gave words on paper to my thoughts while listening to Vivaldi's *Four Seasons*, I began to realize this rather unoriginal title for these ponderings was to take on a whole new life as well as offering several different perspectives to this experience we rather ineptly entitle 'grief'.

As a bereavement support facilitator and palliative educator for the past twenty five years, I had learned much from the folk who entrusted me with their sometimes intense grief after their loved one had died, or as they were trying to prepare for their loved one to die. After Rick's death, many assumed with all that experience, that somehow my grief would be easier to deal with. Wouldn't that be nice, but what's the saying, "Walk first in my moccasins?"

In the early months of writing there were those "Aha" moments, yet, negotiating through dense fog would have been inexplicably more difficult without those closest to me, stumbling their way through how best to support me.

I would receive phone calls daily from friends and loved ones, which were not only welcomed, but were in fact the very thing that got me through each day.

Whilst reflecting on the past, I thought of my second Valentine's Day without Rick. This was a day that we both considered to be highly overrated, but nevertheless, he would always buy me flowers.

I remember having dinner with six other women whose husbands had died. I didn't know how they felt at the time, yet the 'w' word assigned to us was not a label I relished. We truly enjoyed each other's company. The lovely food or wine we contributed to the table where the best conversations occur was planned with purpose. We discovered a camaraderie known only to those finding their way forward without their husbands. Each of us was in a different season. One of those women echoed what the rest of us had already experienced, that she was coming out of the fog, however, finding life more challenging. A different kind of hunger was brought to the table; that of being able to say our husbands' names, share some precious memories and learn from each other how very different, yet similar our experiences were and would be.

While I saw my soul enter a season of spring, the other seasons were well represented by the other ladies in this eclectic group, two of whom appeared at least to have tried to stay warm in the depths of winter. I remember it well and there are still the occasional snow squalls; maybe there always will be.

Interestingly, on my way to work one morning, Julie Nesrallah on CBC's Friday Morning *Music That Rocks Your World* featured a most bright, crisp, energetic version of Vivaldi's *Summer*. This was simply no coincidence that in the past three days, this music had been woven into my thoughts. Julie introduced the piece by reminding us that this music was one we would never tire of, and I would agree. I cranked up the volume and let it rip. However, while I could embrace some of the energy with which this season was being musically communicated, there was much of that summer, which was for me, still to come.

Having pondered over *That Native Thing, Exploring the Medicine Wheel* by Tim Yearington, he introduces the reader to the multi-faceted meaning and value of the Medicine Wheel, a life compass that helps us find our way using the four directions of east, south, west and north. Each direction in the Medicine Wheel sports a different colour to help define its double entendre meaning: Yellow – East portrays the rising sun of morning; Red – South tells us of the glorious sunsets at late afternoon; Black – West portrays the evening, and White – North points to the late, quieter hours of the deep night. The symbolism of the Medicine Wheel could easily be likened to or given kinship to the brilliant, lazy, melancholy and dark tones and sounds of Vivaldi's *Seasons*. I have encountered two years of seasons and found myself lost at times trying to understand which direction and colour of the Medicine Wheel best describes where I am in this passage I am told is called a journey. Symbolism is sometimes the only language we have to help us understand and come to terms with some of those greater mysteries of life. Seasons, directions, the hour of the day and its colour may be the only tools we will have some days to help us understand who and where we are, especially in grief or at a significant crossroad in our lives.

I was introduced years ago in my palliative care and bereavement work to a tool which has become quite meaningful to me and the co-facilitators of our bereavement support program. It is entitled *Pathways of Grief* co-created by Sandra Elder and Linda Martens. Perhaps one of its greatest virtues for those of us finding our way through grief is that it dispels the linear stages theory and a cookie cutter approach and instead allows for us to be literally all over the map with our responses to the death of someone precious. Paralleling it to Vivaldi's *Seasons*, I see how eventually my grief will follow the different cadences of those seasons, weaving back and forth – in and out as I move forward. "Way to go, Vivaldi!"

I offer some observations then from a seasonal perspective along the uncharted territory of grief. While most of us in the initial days of grief probably find ourselves in the cold, rainy seasons of autumn or winter, it is important to acknowledge that those surviving a death out of a broken relationship might find themselves at first in the promise of spring. For them perhaps, the relief of no more abuse or other negative contributors to lost dreams for that relationship could most easily be their first response to their grief. *"Freedom at last!"* My understanding of their grief experience is such that at some point, they will encounter the other seasons as they honestly work through the challenges associated with those less than love-felt relationships. A good counsellor will allow the passages as they unfold, help them identify the differing emotions attached and equip them to move forward.

For those who enjoyed the more positive and loving times and are trying to make sense of their new lives without their loved one, I *think* I can safely surmise as they are finding their way through the first few months or 100 days of fog, shock, numbness and disbelief, that they discover them-selves in the dead of winter. The promise of spring or summer isn't even on the radar most days. Levels of concentration, memory and clarity may be disturbingly diminished leading to questions of personal sanity. Physical exhaustion could be an unexpected bed partner and for some, longing to dream of their loved one could go unmet. Fourteen months later I had had two all too brief happy dreams about Rick and one terrible one. I con-tinue to wish for the former.

I recall needing to create and hibernate into a place of solace within my living room where I could spend literally hours just sitting and looking out onto our treed, now large for me, acre of property. I still spend many hours there. The harsher moments of bleak weather in 2011 matched my emotional time of winter.

While the warmth of spring approached it took quite a while for me to notice its presence. Once in a while, I could feel it peek its head through the snow, and hope was felt. In the aforementioned *Pathways of Grief*, hope is always on the map and its promise then and now continues to remind me there is something much greater than myself, Rick's untimely death, and how I choose to move forward.

Chapter 2

How on Earth Did We Get Here?

———————————

Anyone who has gone through the death of a loved one understands the importance of telling about the day that person died. Saturday, December 11, 2010 will always stir within me a vivid picture. Often I find myself saying or writing December 10, 2011 and I am not sure what that dyslexia is about. Knowing where best to include my personal account of that day needs to be right. A lot of people died on that date worldwide and it is important to acknowledge that frequency to which we have become almost desensitized; however, for me, Rick Bear's death demands to be honoured by its telling.

For two months leading up to that day, Rick had been intensely involved in our high school musical *Beauty and the Beast*, with two other co-directors. Copious hours were spent in auditions, rehearsals, set design, lighting and sound equipment – on top of teaching every day. He and I had somewhat resignedly become used to the demanding pace from September through December each year.

I attended the first performance on Thursday, December 8. A dinner theatre was arranged which went extremely well, but we knew there were still three more performances, which was quite an undertaking for a small school. Friday night's performance, which I did not attend, was ticking along fairly well until there was a major sound glitch. So many people commented after the fact how calmly and adeptly Rick went about determining the source of the problem then correcting it, but I, his wife, know how very long and gut wrenching for him those less than ten minutes would have been. Problem solved, the show went on.

We had thought well ahead that year and gone Christmas tree hunting the Saturday before for, which I heard myself giving thanks many times the rest of the season. Our family absolutely loved having our tree early in December so we could enjoy it late at night and first thing in the mornings while it was still dark outside. Rick got to enjoy our last tree together for one full week.

Saturday morning, December 11. A busy day ahead. Our plan was to shampoo the living room carpet in preparation for our four grandbabies crawling around over the holidays. It was our turn to have our family together under our roof. My part of the bargain was to make sure the machine was in order and that we had carpet shampoo, which we discovered that morning I had overlooked. It was my job to rush downtown and buy the shampoo while Rick moved furniture and vacuumed. In hindsight, bad idea.

When I returned moments later, Rick was just finishing up and I started to get things in order to begin the shampoo task. I was hooking up the yards and yards of hose to our bathroom sink when he came down the hall, into our bedroom saying he was not feeling at all well. A most pasty, sweaty complexion and complaint of chest pains hastened me to call 911 with his permission. With the call made and him very quietly laying on my side of the bed obviously in pain, Rick looked most intently at me and said, "Just in case, I love you."

I bent down, took his face in my hands, kissed his lips and replied, "It's going to be okay." Whether through ignorance, magical thinking or what, I truly thought he had pulled a muscle and just needed to rest, and yet 911 was my first thought when I saw his face.

The whole 'time standing still thing' is a vivid memory. It seemed like forever for fire and ambulance to arrive and yet I think it was truly just minutes. Public school friends of our boys, Jason and Rodney, were two of the first responders. How odd to see those young men in our home for this reason. To this day, there is still in my night table one of the little circle chest pads from the ECG paramedics ran on Rick.

The next six hours of that Saturday were spent at our local hospital where I was most frustratingly prohibited from being with Rick for the first hour, even after I had made three requests to be with him. A follow up letter to the hospital a month later invited them to consider the value of a caregiver's presence during what was reported later as routine tests. I knew there was something seriously wrong with Rick. My gut and palliative training were telling me that there was no reason for me not to be with him to provide calm and a wife's perspective. (That letter is included at the end of this chapter.)

After several hours of less than stellar pain and symptom management and not getting conclusive answers, we were sent to a larger hospital for a CT scan. Again, I was not able to accompany Rick in the ambulance, but a wonderful nurse did. My friend Carole and I arrived to the diagnostic imaging floor sometime between 9 and 9:30 pm. The first angiogram attempt for Rick was not successful, so I waited by his side for the second attempt, remarking to his nurse that his blood pressure seemed to be all over the map. After the second angiogram, the radiologist quickly reported with precise but compassionate delivery that Rick had an aortic dissection requiring immediate open heart surgery, but we needed to consent to a third angiogram to determine whether it was an A or B dissection. We also needed to consent right away to the surgery.

The very last words out of my husband's mouth were: "We place ourselves in your hands." *What trust!* But again, he knew a *lot* earlier in the day than I did how very serious this was. Seconds later Rick's hands did something very strange, awkward and childlike across his chest; his eyes rolled back and the radiologist used words like 'seizing' and 'crashing'.

I leaned over him, touched his face and his hair and called to him, "No, Rick, don't do this, don't leave me." Literally all hell broke loose, Code Blue was called. Just like in the movies, a team of people and machines and instruments came charging down the hall and equally, quickly, they raced Rick down to the ER.

"Mrs. McBay, you need to come with me," asserted an attendant.

"But I need to be with my husband."

"No, you need to come with me now." Carole and I were escorted to a quiet room and left there.

Where was the social worker or chaplain, the obligatory person of calm to be with us while we waited? I wondered. I quickly phoned my sons to beckon them to my side because their dad had seized and crashed. Carole and I did not see anyone until Rick's nurse from Grimsby came into the room, about twenty minutes later. Strongly but quietly I said to her, "I get the fact that you do not need a distraught wife in ER in this kind of situation, but I am not one of those distraught wives and I need to be with my husband, now."

Ever so gently, perhaps with her hand in mine, I don't remember, she looked at me and said, "Sandy, he died." Three little words.

It took my boys considerably less than the allotted one and a half hour's drive to arrive at the hospital. Our minister Noel, my funeral director and friend Ralph, and some other dear friends had already joined me. They exited when Brian and Terral arrived, and at that moment I fell into my sons' arms, sobbing and apologizing for calling them too late. We went down the hall together to have some time with Rick where Noel joined to pray with us. Both boys touched their dad, kissed him and Terral left on his chest a gloriously crafted paper snowman that granddaughter Leah made for her Papa.

Sudden, traumatic death is so very different from expected death due to protracted illness. I wish not to get into a spitting contest around which is worse – they are just vastly different. Disbelief has been my greatest descriptor since December 11, 2010. Even now, I look at my husband's picture in the living room and wonder why he is not sitting beside me in his chair. I go to bed every night and awake each new morning without Rick, and it doesn't compute. As much as I have cringed from that nauseating platitude (one of many), "It just takes time to heal", there is absolute frustrating truth to that. As is there truth to, "He is no longer in any pain." But when that is offered most of us left behind in bereavement realize the truth of that platitude rather invalidates what we are experiencing as we try to move forward. And yet in Rick's case, perhaps the most unwanted outcome was indeed best for him. We heard right after he died about a U.S. senator who also suffered an aortic dissection around that same time; he underwent twenty hours of surgery, and still died. My first thought was, *I would not have wanted Rick to have experienced twenty hours of surgery. And what if he had survived it? What possible quality of life would have been his?* Obviously, answers my family and I will never know. The timing of Rick's death continues to be a mystery to me and yet I am at peace with his final destination.

April 12, 2011
West Lincoln Memorial Hospital
Grimsby, ON
Dear _____

My husband Rick McBay died most unexpectedly on December 11, 2010 from an aortic dissection at the Hamilton General Hospital. 'We' received care first in the West Lincoln ER from approximately 12:40 through 19:00 pm.

I have had four months to reflect on what happened and recently purchased Rick's ER record from West Lincoln Medical Records. Because I believe there is 'always' something to learn from life and death experiences, I offer the following observations to the physician and nurses who cared for Rick. My involvement in palliative care over the past twenty-five years in our community also compels me to do so.

While I have learned and appreciate the difficulty of diagnosing an aortic dissection, I have two concerns I would like to cite. Overall, I know that Rick received compassionate care, but here are my two greatest concerns:

1. The amount of time I was restricted from being with Rick once he arrived at West Lincoln was a full hour in which I respectfully asked three times to be with him but was denied. My presence during routine, non-invasive procedures of blood work, X-rays and general intake would have provided a calming influence for Rick, supporting the well-known concept that the patient as a unit of care includes a family member. Once I was finally 'allowed' to be with Rick as his advocate, I was able to ask for Ativan when he needed it, monitor his pain, massage his cold feet and just quietly 'be' with him.

2. Pain Management in acute or palliative situations is the hallmark of good care. With Rick, I am aware that he vomited quite promptly after his first dose of morphine, which caused some adjustments to the original plan of 1 to 2 mg of morphine every fifteen to thirty minutes. And, I was aware that the nurse somewhat routinely asked Rick his 'pain number'. However, gaps of over one hour in some cases seemed to deviate from that original plan and at one point in the afternoon Rick quietly asked me why 'we' had to ask for more pain meds. He was also quite aware of the vacillations in his heart rate.

Perhaps it is here that I need to say again: the purpose of my letter is not one of setting out to 'get anyone' but to remind us all that patient care includes the family and consistent pain management. And in fact, the calming presence of family can also lead to that consistent management of the patient's 'total' pain.

Part of my grief and coming to terms with this most unexpected death is that I could not be with Rick during some pretty critical times that most memorable day.

Finally, I wish to commend most highly the nurse who accompanied Rick from West Lincoln to the Hamilton General. Her compassionate care of Rick and her 'most' sensitive way of informing me Rick had died will stay with me for a lifetime.

My hope is that my letter will be considered and shared as an opportunity for greater learning and a reminder of good pain management, and that the patient as a unit of care will often include family.

Respectfully

Post Script – July, 2013

I informed West Lincoln Memorial Hospital that I was planning to use and publish this letter. Dr. Paul Cano, the Head of ER gave me a most gracious blessing to go ahead.

Chapter 3

Ritual and One Hundred Days

Perhaps because of the work I do, a preoccupation with death has been present for a number of years. I would ponder often who would die first, Rick or I. When it was Rick's turn in my mind, I concluded early there would be some things I would need to do or facilitate in his honour. When those conclusions catapulted abruptly to reality, I was able to stand my ground. Bringing Rick home from hospital the night he died went against hospital protocol but, when one has a funeral director for a dear friend who came to the hospital prepared, we were able to circumvent a ridiculous security rule. One small thing I could accomplish for my husband, *or was it more for me?*

With the help of my sister and my two funeral director friends, we dressed Rick in the suit he wore to both of our sons' weddings and, then placed him in his casket, which was very emotional, however, something I really needed to do. Speaking at his funeral was a no brainer. There was much on my heart and a visceral desire to remind others of his value added to life. 'Value added' is a mantra Rick practiced in just about everything he worked at. I decided contrary to a stand out line Stuart Maclean used in one of his wonderful Saturday morning Vinyl Café radio shows: "You can't choose who is going to guard your history" that I could buoy and protect Rick's history. And, I needed to ask people not to be afraid of me in my new identity as just Sandy McBay. Having my grandbabies present during visitation and the funeral was just such a natural part of the rituals and some precious moments that only children can provide were enjoyed by all.

Much to Ralph and Doug's angst, I requested we have Rick's casket lowered in our presence at the cemetery, to allow those who wished to throw a shovel full of dirt or a flower into the grave. The comic relief was not lost on those huddled in the cold when during his descent; Rick had the last laugh as the casket rubbing against the vault, crreeaaked all the way down. Singing "Jesus Loves Me" was a most unexpected yet natural response out of my mouth.

Having moved through my first year of all four seasons and heard more times than I ever wished, "you just have to get through your first year of firsts" I wish to acknowledge something loud and clear – for me at least. Every new moment of every day without Rick is a first! Two of many realities hit home: one almost immediately; the second, a year later on the morning of December 12, 2011. First, I realized, I am fifty-seven years old and statistics say I could live another thirty years – *by myself!* Then, I woke up that morning a year later and surmised, *Okay, I get to do this all over again.*

Year two felt more challenging, knowing that there was to be no more 'magical thinking' in the way of those wonderful family and friend occasions, and accomplishments without Rick Bear. At the risk of shameless self-pity, it was bloody lonely.

However, I remember back to when I was a little girl and teen, being content, upbeat, and resilient, and wish those not to be lost on me now. Life is precious, evidenced for me in a plethora of ways. I am willing to risk the scorn from some when I state unequivocally that I/we were created by an awesome God whose majesty is evident even in the darkest of corners. God/Creator mastered the seasons, the human breath, the sanctity of life, the wonder of big and small, the beauty of colour, music and *love*. And as my second minster Dylan states: "Love Wins."

While I might not possess the most acute understanding of the Bible and I would probably lose hands down in a Science vs. God debate, I have seen enough over my almost fifty-eight years of life to know that the two can walk hand in hand, quite amiably. Rick Bear taught me lots about faith, rising above one's circumstances and to believe that no matter what, God is at my side. Fifteen months in retrospect, though not always felt, I had no doubt of God's presence in my life, and His footprints are real.

That morning, a new question entered my mind. I had documented elsewhere that the morning Rick was clearly in trouble, he knew without a doubt that his life was threatened. "Just in case, I love you," visits me every day. *What did he say to God throughout the rest of that day?* I have taught often that when someone is close to death, they will, to the distress of loved ones, withdraw into themselves and into their pain if that is a part of it. I saw Rick do that and yet at the time I did not know he was working on dying. I ponder his prayers that day and wonder many times what he is now experiencing.

Early in our grief my young family had a conversation. I don't recall where the question was raised: "What if Dad is experiencing us right now, every day on some level we simply can't understand? It couldn't possibly be heaven if he saw us in our pain missing him so much. So what is he experiencing?"

We were led to a book called *Heaven is a Place on Earth* by Michael Wittmer, which has joyfully assuaged my concern around the potential of becoming bored in heaven. This was not a concern I had ever expressed to anyone in the event it was considered blasphemous, so when I read Wittmer pen almost exactly the same fear of boredom, I was relieved. And without dangerously understating the premise of his book, it was refreshing to hear his thoughts on heaven actually being a completely restored, renewed earth creation to be celebrated, and not a bunch of clouds upon which to perch and sing praise hymns all day long. (Apologies to Michael Wittmer.)

A recent palliative volunteer in service, I was asked to conduct focusing on bereavement support concerns, which identified some important personal truths, not only for me as facilitator, but for those attending. Volunteers wanted to know how better to support the families they serve after the loss of their loved ones. In addition to the more academic learning I knew was being sought, a memorial ritual for us to close our time together came to mind immediately. Each person was asked to bring a strip of fabric, preferably from the garment of a 'passed' loved one. My vision of weaving these fabric pieces into a communal loom looked far more idyllic in my mind than when it came time to create the loom. Plans A, B and C went quickly out the window leading to the purchase of a grape vine wreath, to which folks could weave or tie their fabric to the wreath in memory of their loved one.

The evening went well I guess. My apprehension was somewhat evident in my occasional loss of thought and uncertainty around a couple of questions raised. To my surprise, a couple of people complimented me from the perspective that this was the first time they had seen me come across more real, not so polished, and in control. Grief shared became grief understood. But I wondered then what I had been projecting in the past, since being 'real' was I thought a part of who I was.

Perhaps a part of the challenge was in the fact that not everyone in the group was bringing a fresh loss to death, which is quite different from the groups I had been facilitating for over twenty years. Though each person's loss is unique to them, the groups establish quickly the safety of common ground and the willingness to listen and learn from each other. I am thankful for the lesson.

Back to Antonio Vivaldi for a moment. My morning coffee (without Rick Bear) was graced one day with one of those brief but magical snowfalls, the kind that reminds one of a child's snow globe where when shaken, the big fat flakes descend ever so gently. Being just weeks away from spring, winter had revisited that morning and it was not as dark, cold and intense as it could be at times. There is absolute beauty in every season, which Vivaldi captured so very well. *Can it be that there is absolute beauty too in these seasons of grief? Will that become more evident with the simple passing of time as we find our way through this uninvited event? Will we see that beauty more clearly once we are at a greater place of strength and looking back?*

I was led to a book called *The Year of Magical Thinking* by Joan Didion, and like Jerry Sittser's *A Grace Disguised*, I couldn't put it down. It would be so much easier if those not walking our path would read some of these writings so they would better understand what we in grief can't seem to find the words to describe. But why would someone want to read such material when they are not personally immersed in the quagmire? This is akin to our palliative volunteer organization's frustration around the fact that many years later, people are still not aware we exist. Their answer when we ask how they did not know about us is often something like, "Why would I want to know about such a service when I don't need it?" In other words, ". . . please don't knock on that door just yet".

Due to the suddenness of her husband's death, Didion was echoing so much of what I had tried to negotiate since December 11, 2010. *Or was I echoing her experience?* The word 'disbelief' stayed with me in a most intense way for months; it's still there at times. Her magical thinking concept was fascinating and true to the experience of most of us I expect. While we know on some level our loved one is not coming back, the intricacy with which our thoughts can trick us into thinking: *When I wake up, this will all have been a very bad dream,* can be most beguiling and unnerving. While I know that I will never go to sleep or wake up with Rick beside me, I will never enjoy morning coffee in the living room with him, and my grandbabies will find it very difficult to remember their Papa other than from pictures, there's still that desire to wake up from the bad dream.

Chapter 4

God's Presence and Goodness since

December 11, 2010

Mid-January of 2011, I was approached gently and respectfully by a sister church in our community to come and speak about Rick's death and where I was finding myself at that time. The desire was for people to hear of someone's personal experience, what they could learn to help others and to understand where God was for me. It was very easy for me to say yes. The following is that presentation with meaningful hymns woven into its progression. While I was speaking a photo of Rick was behind me on a large screen.

Hymn – 'Just As I Am'

"I requested that hymn because it spoke to me most strongly during my more initial journey as a younger Christian and because we just don't sing it anymore. But it is such a wonderful description of redemption, surrender, promise and coming to the Lamb of God for love and solace.

"This will be kind of a fireside chat – I will be fairly candid because I truly hope this will be of help to others finding their way after the death of someone precious and to those of you supporting them. My brother-in-law Doug also helped me clarify that no, I don't want you to feel sorry for me; I want you to understand – even a little bit.

"After I called 911 with Rick's blessing, he looked at me with unsettling intent and said, 'Just in case, I love you.' My assurances that everything would be all right I truly believed. I had not grasped as he had so quickly, the seriousness of what was happening.

"The nurse who travelled with Rick by ambulance from Grimsby to the Hamilton General came in to the 'quiet room' to where my dear friend Carole and I had been whisked away after Rick crashed, Code Blue was called and he was taken to ER. She very gently looked at me and quietly said, 'Sandy, he died.'

"When asked what I would have done differently had I known that morning that Rick would have been dead by 9:50 that night, I would have touched him more and sang to him gently, 'Have I told you lately that I love you?' That song, sung originally by Van Morrison became 'our song'. We would request it at weddings and bathe in its reminder while dancing ever so close. In fact, I treasured the importance of that song for us so much that I had my neighbour/metal sculptor friend Floyd; create for Rick one Christmas a decorative metal musical staff with the first ten notes to the song included. It graces the outside back wall of our garage and is visible from our living room.

"I still struggle with the fact that I had spent the past eight months taking a most intensive, personal course on contemplative end of life care and couldn't put what I had learned into practice. When thrown most unexpectedly into this life threatening situation that I didn't know was life threatening, that education somehow got lost. I am working with my family doc on the fact that I was kept from being with Rick when he first arrived at hospital and that my requests to be present seemed to fall on protocol instead of the value of a loved one providing a calming presence.

"Quite quickly after Rick died, Noel arrived and I was able to say with absolute confidence, "Imagine what Rick is seeing right now." His Dad Russ, arrived fairly quickly after that as did Ralph and Laurena Tallman. As soon as my boys arrived, they all quietly left the room and I had to tell Brian and Terral I had called them too late and their Dad had died. After feeling quite helpless all day without knowing the severity of the situation, until just a few moments before Rick died, there was one thing I could do for him, which I pursued with great determination. That was to bring Rick home to Vineland instead of leaving him unnecessarily in the Hamilton Hospital morgue. When Ralph and Laurena arrived, I asked if they just happened to bring a van. Laurena said with a most timely impish smile, 'Maybe.' My determination with the ER charge nurse prevailed and my very emotional funeral director friend Ralph made the final arrangements to honour my request and bring Rick home.

"'O give thanks to the Lord for he is good, for His steadfast love endures forever.' **(Psalm 107)**

"My purpose this evening is to give testimony as to God's goodness despite painful times and struggles. The list is long. But I am also here to just simply tell you what it is like for me and my family and to solicit your understanding of us, who I believe some now avoid.

"'God is our refuge and strength, a very present help in trouble. Therefore we will not fear, though the earth should change, though the mountains shake in the heart of the sea; though its waters roar and foam, though the mountains tremble with its tumult . . . be still, and know that I am God! I am exalted among the nations; I am exalted in the earth.' **(Psalm 46)** These few verses were read by Dylan Pyeatt as he opened up a completely altered plan of worship at our Tintern church Sunday morning after Rick died, so to give people opportunity to sing, pray and say what they needed to about Rick. I have listened to that time of worship three times and I am comforted by God's presence for my church family that morning. 'For His steadfast love endures forever.'

"God's goodness was in the wisdom behind the Great Lakes Christian High School staff to gather Sunday evening for a time of supportive devotion and to plan a two-hour assembly the following morning before they could even consider classes beginning. Staff and students together sang, prayed and testified to their respect and love for Rick.

"'O taste and see that the Lord is good; happy are those who take refuge in Him.' **(Psalm 34)**

"YOU ARE MY GOD YOU ARE MY KING

You are my God, You are my King

You are my Master, my everything

You are my Lord, that's why I sing to You

Hallelujah, Hallelujah **(Delavan, 1984**

"God's gifts of strength continued to flow in the hearts of my boys and my daughters-in-law as they tried almost desperately to do whatever they could to help me while trying to figure things out for themselves and my grandbabies. My brother and sister's presence provided familial stability and their gracious acts of welcome to people waiting in line for more than an hour during visitation were a most loving means of support. My desire to dress Rick and help place him in his casket was hesitantly honoured by Ralph and Doug and again, God walked me through this loving task with my sister's help.

"The most incredible presence of so many during visitation was truly overwhelming for us as a family, but oh so comforting. A Great Lakes student fell into my arms and sobbed as he approached the casket. Our family doc and his wife Mary were one of many who waited in line at visitation and Seamus was able to speak with many of my family and help them understand just what happened to Rick. How many docs do that these days?

"'For His steadfast love endures forever...'

"The collective desire of my boys, girls and I to have a funeral full of singing, memories, worship and acknowledgement of grief was completely honoured, the only greater impact being its attendance. There were literally hundreds of people I had no idea were present. I believe many may have needed to be there to witness a real God being honoured in the remembrance of one who sought to glorify Him as best he could. Whatever Rick was doing during that almost two hours, he and Jesus had to have been impressed. As my brother surprisingly and eloquently stated, we were all the voice of Rick that day and I concluded, surely the presence of the Lord was in that place.

"*SURELY THE PRESENCE*

Surely the presence of the Lord is in this place

I can hear his mighty power and His grace

I can feel the brush of angel's wings; I see glory on each face

Surely the presence of the Lord is in this place.
(Wolfe, 1977)

"Perhaps it is here I would like to pass on some words of encouragement to families with little children. Brian and Shanna were truly uncertain what to do about having their children involved with the funeral. At first they had decided against much involvement and I listened without response. As discussions began to unfold, Shanna approached me and said, 'Okay, this is part of what you do, should we have Carter and Haley at the visitation and funeral?' Here again is where God gently led us forward and we were able to agree that yes, this is a part of life, we are family, and children should not be left out. My work over the years and hearing stories of regret from so many has convicted me in this matter. I say to all of you, when you are faced with a family funeral where little children may be involved, include them as much as you can without forcing them. They will appreciate it years later.

"'For His steadfast love endures forever...'

"I recall gathering all of our family and extended family together before the funeral began and asked them to be okay with me needing quiet time to myself for a few days afterwards. While the bountiful acts of love and support were ones I did not want to see end, I was also feeling an almost desperate need for time alone. I knew I would be okay. "Being still and knowing I am God" was where I needed to be to help me begin to understand all that happened.

"Many hours have been spent in quiet from my living room, which has been rearranged to facilitate being still and watching the birds. I have to remember it is now my job to feed them. Some of those hours cannot be accounted for other than to say I knew God was with me most times, yet uncertain of His presence at other times. Laurena shared with me that my somewhat emotional voice mail I had left she and Ralph asking them to come to the hospital because Rick had died, caused an almost guttural response in Ralph she never wanted to hear again. My pain seems to be shared by many.

"Over the past three months, I have received three different flower arrangements from an anonymous carer. The card simply reads each time; *God rejoices over you with gladness,*' from Zephaniah 3:17. While I have some ideas who the surprising giver may be, I can't be sure, but I confess it was the first time I became aware there was even a book in the Bible entitled Zephaniah. God continues to teach through others.

"As well, among the hundreds of cards, some of them including memories of Rick, I have received three hand written notes on special paper from Jan Taylor recounting some wonderful memories she had of Rick over the years – one quite touching, the other two – laugh out loud stories. The fact that she took the time to do that in the lost art of the hand written note is extremely precious and helpful.

"My sister and two sisters'-in-law call me almost daily, as do Laurena and my lifelong friend Deb. While it is difficult on both sides to know what best to say each time, that regular checking in with me has been most appreciated, therapeutic and yet another reminder of God's arms wrapping me and holding me close.

"January 22 was Rick's birthday and my family and I spent that weekend together. With four grandbabies three years and under, it was a wild and crazy time. Nana bought nine helium balloons to be released at the cemetery on the coldest day yet this winter. We had not included our children at the burial, so there was building angst as to just how we were going to explain what we were doing. As Brian and I were getting out of the car, he turned to me with a most pained look on his face and said, 'Mum.' I didn't let him finish and said, 'Don't worry, we aren't going to do anything but release our balloons and yell Happy Birthday, Papa!' We did, we watched them fly away and quickly returned to our cars. On warmer spring or summer days when we can plant some sunflowers at Papa's grave, we can begin simple conversations with our babies around death and burial.

"Work has been a needed source of structure. Staff and students have been more plentiful with much appreciated hugs. Some bittersweet moments continue to occur with Russ Walker helping the Great Lakes chorus move forward and me being present during practices. Other than some challenges of students focusing and listening, Rick would be quite proud.

"Rick taught my boys well in his own quiet way. Plus, I think they needed time with me as much as I needed time with them. On Valentine's Day I was an extremely proud mother who was taken for supper by her sons, given long-stem roses and a picture created by my grandbabies. The three of us commented the next day that none of us wanted them to return home that night and yet their Momma was concerned about them driving too late after an already long day. So there was this emotional tug of war and the silent grief palpable.

"An unfolding meaning of Rick's death comes in the form of lovely, unanticipated extensions of love and support. One of our international students makes sure he gives me a hug and checks in with me each time he sees me. Once we encountered each other in the stairwell and I suggested that maybe that wasn't the best place for a student and staff member to be hugging. A young woman I found a little more difficult to know initially has discovered many little ways to let me know how much she cares and also misses Rick. She and her mother are most concerned, as am I, about my gardens and they have asked if they can give me a hand.

" '*For His steadfast love endures forever...*'

"Perhaps it is here again that I shed some light on what it is like for someone like me and how you can best support me and my family. Apparently I am now a 'widow', a label I find annoying and almost insulting. Asking 'how are you', or 'how are you really?' while perhaps well intentioned is an impossible question to answer, at least right now. And I would suggest that unless you really do care to know, maybe a better greeting would simply be a hug and 'it's good to see you'. As my boys, girls and I chart this new territory, simply checking in with us and offering practical means of support and a willing listening ear over coffee would be most welcome. Please know also, that we are not afraid to talk about Rick and in fact welcome those opportunities. We are still trying to get our heads around the fact that he is not coming back. It has been interesting to hear some speculate that because I have worked in the area of bereavement I will be better equipped than most to move forward. While an intriguing theory, it's not so much in practice. The numbness is wearing off, I am getting used to being alone, I'm not afraid of that but hate its reality. I still love to laugh, but my quiet times at home or when I least expect it in the car can be filled with sobs of grief and the fact that I miss Rick very much. However, even then or maybe mostly then is when God is close by. '*For His steadfast love endures forever...*'

"While unsettling and most annoying, a leaky basement can bring out the best in people. Not only did it afford another most wonderful and

25

needed alone time with Brian and Terral one Friday night, it rallied the troops and brought several men into my home on a late Saturday night, each equipped with shop vacs and ready to help. They created a schedule for sucking up the water all night and I went to bed. Because I have always believed that God works through His people, we continue to be incredibly blessed.

"As I said at the beginning, the list of God's blessings to me is long and I have just scratched the surface, but I so appreciate being able to tell some of the story.

"*For His steadfast love endures forever.*'"

Chapter 5

One Year: December 11, 2011

Remembering Rick Bear

_____

There are many out there who have counselled (with love I know) that it's the first year of *firsts* that's the worst. For the record, every new moment without Rick is a first and will continue to be, although with diminishing capacity over time, I know.

Saturday morning over coffee, I look at Rick's picture and ask, "Where the ___ are you, Rick?" Saturday morning coffees not only got him through each busy week but connected our love on such a quiet and deep level. Over the years, we were arriving at a place in our relationship where quiet was okay, the shared 'knowing looks' were becoming plentiful and we were more comfortable in our shared skin.

A year after my husband's death, I questioned where we were as a family. While I can't be too specific in terms of how my children and grandchildren think, I asked myself: *Where am I, and who am I?* Wow, most days I had *no* idea and had been almost suffocated at times by that question. And yet, as I said to my Great Lakes colleagues recently in appreciation of all they have done for me, there was a light growing inside of me, even if I was not sure yet where the light was taking me.

I bought a book that had been enthusiastically recommended to me by a friend and bereavement colleague: *A Grace Disguised* by Jerry Sittser. Having started reading the book, I was immediately engrossed, reflecting on some of his thoughts in comparison to my own.

Every single day of that year had been a rehearsal of December 11, 2010. Much of grief is that way, accompanied by the almost insatiable need to tell the story often, with the hope that, somehow, it will all make sense.

When Rick seized and crashed at the hospital, it could have been an episode from a traumatic medical TV show. Literally, all hell broke loose, people running, racing Rick down the hall to the trauma room, one man wanting to escort me to the quiet room and I not wishing to be too terribly compliant because I wanted to be with Rick.

The fact that my friend Carole was with me was beyond providential as the nurse gently came in to the quiet room 20 minutes later and ever so softly told me Rick had died. If that wasn't difficult enough to try to take in, probably the most impossible thing I had done in my then 56 years of life was to tell Brian and Terral when they arrived that I had called them too late. I had never cried like that with my boys before. The almost symmetry of our minister Noel, his dad Russ and my funeral directors Ralph and Laurena showing up at the hospital was not lost on me either. We were able to bring Rick 'home' that night instead of him having to stay needlessly in that hospital morgue.

I do not believe I have challenged God once with this personal tragedy, but He has certainly heard my laments. I have been enveloped in His love through the myriad of demonstrations of love and support from others – many so very dear and a few rather pleasantly unexpected. One Saturday, I came home to a bouquet of flowers and a card from a neighbour I personally had not met but knew Rick. I dropped by their home on my way to church the next morning to thank them and to simply ask, "Why?" She recalled being at our neighbour Floyd's Artifice Open House that day and seeing the ambulance come to the house. She just wanted me to know she remembered that. *Wow*!

Rather early on, I had a fleeting dream of Rick, the kind you wished would last ever so much longer. He was getting out of an old Volkswagen van in our driveway to which I joyfully exclaimed, "You've come back!" and then he was gone. I don't know how many people had told me over that year of their dreams about Rick but I had been becoming increasingly ticked that I had not . . . until the second dream, and it was *not* pleasant.

While I do not put a huge amount of stock in dreams, Terral and I wondered if my frustrations needed to find a place of release.

As this grief thing had been increasing in intensity, it had manifested itself to a feeling of trying to juggle a whole lot of balls and just barely keeping them all in the air. And yet, there had been days when I had worked outside, realizing I had done many jobs Rick would have done, and the accomplishment had been visceral, emotional and created a wonderful moment of peace.

I had frustrated some of my closer friends by not being able to describe what this has been like for me and how specifically they could help. They continued to be awesome in trying.

My boys, girls and grandbabies: I think we had been more careful of each other than perhaps we needed to be. And yet, I became aware early, as did they, that the differences in our relationships with Rick would dictate absolute differences in how we grieved. I also speculated (I believe correctly) that the busyness of their lives with their little families and more would somehow put aside their grief at times. Whereas, I lived with the obvious absence of Rick every day. The other speculation I had was that their grief would surface more significantly at that time of year and I had been hearing that early on from my Shanna and Laura. While we had all been stopped in our tracks by Rick's most untimely death for different reasons over that first year, it was only natural that tension had been mounting in anticipation of December 11, 2011. We remembered Rick at church with apple pie (his favourite) and my boys helped in the leading of worship.

Perhaps one of the most regular gut wrenching things that caused us all to flinch, perhaps even curse, was when one of my sweet grandbabies – Carter, Leah, Haley or Seth reached a little milestone: Seth's first steps, Carter's first day at school, Leah's phone call to say that she was using the potty, or Haley's discoveries of anything 'princess'. *Did Rick see or experience these on some level? Did he need to?* A big question for our family had been: "What if he is experiencing us still in some way that we cannot possibly fathom, yet he is not seeing us struggle?" *Heaven Is a Place On Earth* by Michael Wittmer, has some interesting, scripture based thoughts on that that have comforted to me.

So, how would I get to a place where my memories of Rick would somehow sustain me? I rather he was here. I guess that's because it would simply just take time for the wonderful memories to comfort rather than torment. Sorrow would become a part of a healthier me, however, there are so many moments when feeling sorrow and joy are simultaneous. My soul is growing bigger in response to that pain – or as Rick Bear would say (*and it would drive me crazy!*), my character was being built.

I was beginning to recognize my ability to come out of this deep loss, licking and healing my wounds, to acknowledge other people's loss – although it was less than perfect. My dearest friend Debby, whose daughter Carey died two months before Rick, had learned better than I to check in. While our losses were significantly different, our fifty-year friendship had laid the foundation for sharing our grief. She is a hero to me (yes, we use that word too often but it is appropriate here). I recall phoning Deb a lifetime ago after I had seen the movie *Beaches* and heard Bette Midler's song *Did You Ever Know That You're My Hero?* I said something sappy like, "That song was written about you."

Arlene and Byron's son Jeremy, a friend to my sons Brian and Terral, died one month and two days before Rick. Arlene and I learned to support each other through Facebook. While I had worked in bereavement support for almost eighteen years, this was now *very* personal and I understood on a much more guttural level what this had been like for others. My radar was being honed so I could reach out and apply more meaningful support.

For my sons, daughters and grandbabies: I wondered how we had been able to do this? My desire was for us to be a little more open and real with each other but I think time with busy little families was our greatest enemy. I invited them to communicate more, with me, with each other – especially through writing, Skype or phone since we didn't get as much face-to-face as we would have benefited from. My love was and is so encompassing, I prayed the differences we sometimes discover would never get in the way of our family unit.

Carter, Leah, Haley and Seth – your discovery of life (like little sponges) each second of the day brings me incredible joy. Thank you and Nana loves you.

Rick Bear – I hate this. I miss you every moment. I lament not loving you sometimes the way you needed. I miss everything about you, even the annoying stuff. Our relationship was not perfect as relationships go. *Am I angry with you for leaving?* I don't know how to answer that.

I miss future opportunities to sit with you in the living room, by our gardens, on our swing, on the dock welcoming the loons. Thank you for your steelish faith in our maker God. Maybe that faith is why I have not felt the need to challenge God. I don't know how to by myself, offer counsel when our children may need it, hence I put my foot in my mouth sometimes. But I will continue to learn.

Christmas was coming; a couple of pretty sad attempts at lights were put up by me until a most unexpected gift from our boys on that Saturday. While I was being kept away by some devious friends, Brian, Terral, Carter and Leah came to do some clean-up work in Nana's yard and created a beautiful display of lights with a resurrected family painted wood ornament of carollers, to which *you* would respond by saying, "Awesome, but what about those three bulbs that are crooked?"

I awaited our two little families to arrive that Friday night when we would get the kids to bed then watch the funeral service – for them, that was to be the first time. Saturday morning we would go find the best tree ever for Nana's house. I couldn't wait to sit in the dark with just the tree lights on, being accompanied by some of our glorious Christmas music. *But how on earth did I do that without you?*

You are loved and sometimes I think we will be okay . . .

Chapter 6

Bereavement Support:

The Personal and the Academic

While not at all original, grief is messy. Too many theorists over the years whose intent was to make the experience more manageable, have confused us more and our comfort level with those in grief doesn't seem to have improved all that much.

Over the past seventy plus years, society has sanitized death, dying and bereavement. Death as natural, death in the home with family all around, death as a part of community somehow took a very bad rap and was handed over to the hospitals and long term care facilities, otherwise known as the professionals. Public grief and mourning became feared and, "We best not include the children!" *How tragic!*

When I was a little girl, having funerals and burials for bugs, frogs and little birds was such a natural response within me. I could be quite dramatic about it all but my little rituals gave me comfort. But when my grandfathers and two dear uncles died before I was the age of ten, I was not included in any of those important rituals, and that just didn't seem right. When it came time to bury my best friend Lee at the tender age of twenty (after walking alongside her for ten years as she struggled with cancer), this was my first experience with a funeral, it was foreign territory and all such an unnecessary shame.

The hospice movement over the past forty years has worked hard to de-sanitize the death experience and remind us that while there may be thanatologists and experts at end of life, families remain – in my mind at least – the best experts. And yet there is still much for us to re-learn. This was evidenced by my own local hospital not being comfortable to allow me to be with Rick for his first hour of hospitalization and the second hospital shooing me away when my gut told me being at his side was where I needed most to be. Death *is* tragic, unpredictable in its final hours or moments but far more frightening when patient and caregiver are separated; one left to exit life on his own and the other left to *her* own imagination.

We ponder in our palliative classes about whether a person should ever die alone and I do believe some people, by choice, do desire that preference for a host of reasons. I am not so sure though that in sudden situations like Rick's that that is the time to worry how family may deal, or not, with the rapidly unfolding trauma. Perhaps ER staff would vehemently disagree, but my soul mate of almost thirty-six years died without me at his side. We were the only ones familiar to each other in a most unfamiliar, life ending event. And we were both frightened. We promised in sickness and health, until death parted us. I remember when another palliative colleague drew my attention to a study documented in the New York Times looking into the value of family members being present with their loved one in traumatic situations (*The New York Times* Online – March 14, 2013): "It seems counterintuitive: allowing family members of deathly ill patients to watch while doctors try to restart the patients' hearts. Wouldn't it be traumatic for the family to see? Couldn't it be distracting for the doctors? But a new study, the largest rigorous trial on this issue to date, has found that family members who observed resuscitation efforts were significantly less likely to experience symptoms of post-traumatic stress, anxiety and depression than family members who did not."

I have included another perspective I received from a young woman named Heather.

"When my grandmother was dying, her children established a schedule so she was never alone. My one aunt expressed her great discomfort – she felt it stripped her mother of her dignity for her children and grandchildren to see her in that condition. She stated, 'I do not want any of you doing this for me.' But thinking of the alternative – my Grandma inching toward death without the physical comfort of love in the room breaks my heart and I'm glad the vigil continued. I also know the gift to the family it is to surround someone as she breathes her last – as my husband, his sister, father and I were able to do for his mother."

As much as I hate the reality I now face, death is a part of life, not new under the sun I realize. But what families did together up until about a hundred years ago, made this most important final task of life much more natural, real and perhaps even palatable. For those reading this who are involved in end of life/palliative care, a most beautiful eight-month course is now available out of a small yet noble institution of learning in Toronto, Ontario – the Institute For Traditional Medicine. The 'Contemplative End of Life Care' course, the first in Canada, was an absolute privilege for me to be a part of and we were about the business of re-learning what is important in end of life care. What became a mantra for me was the statement offered the very first weekend by course instructor Dr. Michele Chaban: "We need to get back to the tender art of palliative caring and not just practice the science of palliative medicine."

After twenty five years of the academics of grief and mourning and walking alongside others, Rick's death caused a head on collision with those greater realities I had only been able to empathize. I was unprepared for the very physical response to grief over the first several months. Nor was I prepared for a most bizarre few moments of panic about three weeks after the funeral. On my way to meet my friends Ralph and Laurena for lunch after church, I stopped by the cemetery. It was a particularly cold day. The flowers on the grave had long since frozen and the little black plastic grave marker looked somewhat dwarfed in the snow. My mind suddenly took me to a place of horror, wondering, beginning to panic as to whether Rick was somehow still alive in that box in the cold ground six feet under. "This is crazy," I reminded myself. "You dressed him and put him in the casket, you touched his cold body, he is dead." When I arrived at the restaurant my first words to Ralph were, "I know this is crazy, but you did embalm Rick didn't you?" *Where on earth did that come from?* So much for the learned, experienced bereavement facilitator.

As much as I had preached often that the more difficult work of grief does not happen for most of us until months later, I was unprepared when it arrived. The 'strength' that people saw in me in the beginning dissolved as did I, often, at the most unexpected prompts. Questioning my abilities, my sanity, my persistent desire for solitude within my self-created cocoon was alarming. Again, I was unprepared in the heart for the challenges that year two had assigned. *Where was my boasted resilience?* Was I truly being sucked into the vortex of self-pity or was this normal? I considered when I would stop having to push myself out the door to work, to church, to teach, to be with friends, to visit my two precious families, to enjoy life as it came the way I used to? Who was I at this time?, I wondered.

Dr. David Kuhl, a palliative physician from British Columbia wrote an eye opening book, *What Dying People Want.* I heard him almost apologetically affirm in a TV interview how potentially audacious that title sounds, as if he had become the authority for those at end of life. He addresses well the question of a person's life meaning and how they could possibly answer the question, "Who am I?" Answering this question has been a valuable exercise I include in the palliative training I facilitate and which I answered for myself some years ago. So far, I have been afraid to re-write that.

The first time I had to answer the question "Married or widowed?" I refused the two choices and replied: "I live alone now," and thought to myself, *You can deduce from that whatever you wish.* Men and women whose spouses have died do not need to be reminded on some gov-ernment form of their new status in life. One of my husbandless co-horts, Connie, decided we should call our little single women group the 'Single Roses' (in homage to our Rose Cottage Visiting Volunteers alliance).

As with parents whose child has died, the brother-less sister, the grand-child without the unconditional love of their grandparent . . . we get it. Branding us with an unwanted title which sets us apart seems a bit like overkill. How does the family Christmas card writer sign the card next year? Or what does the couple say at a dinner party when they greet someone new and are asked how many children they have? Do they lie and answer two, leaving out their daughter who died? Should they spoil the party by saying, "We had three children, but our middle daughter died," and then change the subject swiftly?

The most important person in our lives has died and then people become afraid of us. Our circumstances remind them (nowhere near as vividly as with us) that life is fragile, can be much shorter than we ever dreamed and changes in an instant. Well yes, that is frightening. But when we were children and frightened in the dark by that really loud clap of thunder, or the boogey man, what did we want to do? Most people would probably answer they wanted to feel protected, feel close to someone that would help them feel safe and not left alone. Why then, do many people step back just when we the survivor(s) are most vulnerable and alone? Is it because we threaten their homeostasis and remind them that death really is a part of life? What do they say, what can they do, how can they help? So many withdraw and do nothing, hoping that they will be spared an extra month, an extra year, ten, maybe more before they are forced to confront what we have and what is inevitable.

The most important lessons I have learned personally and from the hundreds of people seeking support over the past twenty five years turn out to be far less complicated than we make them. And yet for the person in grief, acknowledging their new circumstances and being supported along the way can make such an incredible difference.

To those brand new to this reality of life after someone precious to you has died and to those a little more seasoned who have weathered the storm over more than a few months:

1. Listen to yourself first. Even though there will be days when you question your own sanity, you are your best expert as to how you are doing. When you are not sure, seek out others who have been where you are, or that one or two most dear friends who know how and wish to listen. For those quick to dispense advice? Smile if you can and say no thank you.

2. Tap into resources you know are dependable and trustworthy.

3. Much of your grief will be a solo flight. When it seems almost more than you believe your resilience can handle, you may need to give in to it. If your personal resources allow, take a pajama day when that happens. If work continues to be absolutely necessary and you need to be fully present to do your job, you may need to request a short medical leave from work to regain the balance. Find other ways to express outwardly all that is going on inside so to release that emotional tension. Writing, journaling, physical activity, music, some form or artistic expression or calling one of those two dear friends (no matter the hour of the day) are some actions you can take.

4. See your physician. Sometimes grief may be very physical. As already mentioned, I have been surprised and sometimes shocked by the magnitude of its physicality. A bout of vertigo rather handily unravelled all my reserves. Vertigo is *not* just dizziness; in fact, describing the sensation is

challenging and there can be significant headache, nausea, real fatigue, compromised cognitive skills and lack of balance. If experienced severely enough, forget driving, forget functioning normally for a time. This time, I could not have expected the bizarre emotional response to the debilitation. From onset through three full days, I simply cried about anything and everything. The symptoms were more pronounced with a few additions. The uncontrollable tears and the accompanying anxiety to those tears exacerbated all the other symptoms to a point I quite literally became very worried something else was at hand, and, I was most upset with myself at the same time. Missing my opportunity to take my granddaughter Leah out to tea with Nana for her fourth birthday then to buy her birthday present did not help matters. Again, I was reminded that I work hard at moving forward without Rick and that portrays outwardly most of the time, a relatively together person. But when illness visits, that together person loses, for a time, their emotional resolve. I am told not to be so hard on myself. For those who can echo what seems for them to be unreasonable physical responses to their grief, I suspect you are not alone. And get it checked out by your doctor!

5. Sorry, you are going to hate this one as much as I have – give yourself time, *lots* of time. No, I don't think it heals but it really is necessary.

To those wanting to know how best to support their friend or loved one who is grieving:

- 1. Talk about the person who died, mention their name, share memories of them.
- 2. Call your friend who is grieving and if you don't know what to say, tell them that. It will level the playing ground. Call regularly.
- 3. Resurrect the diminishing art of the handwritten note. Three different people sent me memories of Rick this way and the care they had taken in choosing the paper, writing the memory and putting it in the mail touched me deeply.
- 4. Offer specific practical support, and follow through. Friends and church folk arranged a roster of men to shovel my driveway the first winter without Rick and ensure a path through my backyard to the woodpile so I could easily gather wood for my living room stove. Two

young men created space in one side of my garage so I could enjoy the luxury of protecting my new to me car from the elements.

- 5. Be okay with the fact that your friend might need to decline a social invitation. But, if they decline too often, check in with them. Maybe they need a gentle nudge.
- 6. Understand the potential for physiological changes in your friend. Exhaustion, lack of sleep, needing to sleep a *lot*, appetite changes, less than stellar levels of concentration and organization, possible anxiety and depression can become strange bedfellows for a while, causing survivors to question their sanity.
- 7. Understand that there is not a cookie cutter approach to grief and mourning. Certainly there will be similarities for all of us but because you don't see your friend responding to their loss in the way you surmise you might respond does not mean it's wrong!
- 8. *Don't* offer platitudes, they are so annoying and thoughtless. Not two weeks after Rick died, a friend of my brother in British Columbia wanted me to know that her dear friend met another man and married him two years after her first husband died, implying that could be possible for me. All I could respond with in as even but deliberate a tone as possible was, "What exactly are you trying to tell me, Whitney?" What I really wanted to scream was, "Honey, you have no idea what you are talking about and how dare you?" Please think before you speak and sometimes it may be better not to say anything at all, especially if you are saying it to make yourself feel better.
- 9. Invite conversation beyond "How are you?" which is almost impossible to answer. Perhaps ask instead, "What has today been like for you?" Be prepared for the answer and be prepared for repetition. Initially we need to tell the story often to help us truly compute what happened and perhaps even why. Listen without trying to fix.
- 10. Invite your friend for coffee or a meal. For those negotiating a spousal death, life at home on their own can be extremely lonely. And for those who weren't the cook in the family, home cooking may be lost on them. Peanut butter and jam is okay but not every night.
- 11. Don't be afraid to include children! At the death bed, in the hospital, and in any funeral/memorial rituals family decides. When my family and I were beginning discussions around visitation and

funeral, I knew my older son Brian and his wife Shanna were really struggling to know what to do with three-year-old Carter and not yet two-year-old Haley. Out of a tender, wise discussion resulting in their more confident decision to have the children present blossomed two precious lifetime memories for all of us. During visitation held at our church, little Leah in her beautiful almost floor length Christmas dress discovered the water cooler and little paper cups. She spent most of the afternoon filling the little cups half full, lining them up on the table beside, and then most carefully walking the full length of the room to bring family and friends a cup of water. "One day children were brought to Jesus in the hope that he would lay hands on them and pray over them. The disciples shooed them off. But Jesus intervened: 'Let the children alone, don't prevent them from coming to me. God's kingdom is made up of people like these.' After laying hands on them, he left." **(Matthew 19: 13-15 – The Message.)** Carter expressed concern several times about how Papa would be able to eat and where he would be able to go potty. When I listened to the audio recording of Rick's funeral the first couple of times, I could not decipher initially why there was a full 2.5 minutes of background noise. Listening more intently, I discovered a tiny little voice ebbing and flowing over the noise. Finally, I realized it was during the family procession behind Rick's casket to the front of the church. The little voice was Carter asking again about Papa in that box and a host of other questions. *Precious!*

- 12. In bereavement support we have learned over the years that the really hard work of grief will ensue for months later. Right at the time when the rest of the world has begun to move forward and resume the status quo, your friend will just be starting to realize – this isn't going away. Each morning they wake up will be one more day without that person. Remind yourself on your calendar to check in with them regularly.

- 13. Remember the anniversary of the death in small but meaningful ways.

- 14. Allow for or invite conversations of forgiveness . . . certainly, there are a number of 'what ifs?' 'should or shouldn't haves' that may need to be spoken, and acknowledged to move forward. Many of those won't necessarily require forgiveness, but some will. If there appears to be a real stumbling block for that friend or loved one grieving, help them seek out the proper helping resources.

- 15. Don't assume that that 'year of firsts' is somehow the magic solution and your friend will wake up day one of year two 'all better'. Depending on a number of variables, each subsequent day, month and year solidifies for your friend that this new normal is here to stay and that can continue to feel foreign, lonely and scary for a long while.

- 16. Along with that 'year of firsts' theory is the much touted idea that not making big decisions during that first year is to be advised. I used to agree with that until I met with men or women who out of no choice of their own *had* to do just that. Think of the young woman who lived with her husband and family on an army base and how she will be expected to vacate in three months. What about the man or woman whose financial situation has changed drastically with the death of their spouse and must move out of that more expensive home or must find a job that demands relocating? Near the end of the first year without Rick, I began to spend a fair bit of money on our house having the septic system inspected, installing new windows and purchasing a new furnace. It made sense at the time to include central air as it would be more expensive later on to do that separately. That was a more emotionally difficult decision to make because Rick and I had never the money to enjoy central air. I suspect some people questioned those large expenses and perhaps surmised that I was going a little crazy with 'the insurance money'. I love our home but it is becoming a whole lot more than I can manage alone so I may have to move sooner than I would like or let this lovely spot become run down. Making some major expenses on the home to maintain its value are actions of good stewardship and prudence, not those of a crazed woman acting hastily.

- 17. Please remember that some people in grief have to take actions like going back to work immediately, out of sheer necessity that may look questionable to their friends. And most places of employment don't honour more than the obligatory three days. My returning to work almost immediately was good and bad. Certainly now, I must continue to work for a while, although our financial planning over our years together resulted in a most pleasant surprise when I sat down with our financial advisor. "Thank you, Rick Bear." Both my boys asked Roger immediately if I was going to be okay and he assured them I would. And Roger had spent many hours reminding me of that as well, but it still requires me working until sixty-five. I returned to Great Lakes three days after we buried Rick. Being close to the students and staff was important and needed, although Rick's absence was tough. Having a focus outside of me was good. But there were a couple of meltdowns over the following months, one of which helped me conclude I needed some time. One afternoon, I turned to my co-worker in an elevating state of anxiety and blurted, "I need to go home, right now." One look at me told her to simply say, "Go, come back when you are able." I visited my doc and requested a brief leave of absence and he gave me a week. I had hoped for two, but the week served me well.

- 18. Counselling or bereavement support groups aren't for everyone but they most certainly do help those who attend. But at the same time, not all groups are created equal. Someone seeking out a group should ask questions, find people who have attended and get their feedback. I have never been convinced that open ended groups work. People need to know there is a beginning and end to a program, that there will be equal opportunity for all participants and that they will leave equipped with some tools to help them continue to move forward.

A word to grandparents – Written January 4, 2013

I visited two friends today who are grandmothers grieving deeply the death of a perfectly formed, full-term grandson in stillbirth. Last night I read requests on Facebook for prayers for two different families who are also experiencing the death of a two-month-old child and another stillbirth. Tomorrow a large community will say goodbye to a ninety-two-year-old wife, grandmother and great grandmother. And we are just four days into a New Year. Not only that, probably every town or city in every country has had a number of losses to death just today for reasons too many to mention.

It continues to be an awe-filled mystery to me this thing we call life. And I am reminded yet again how important it is for us to pause, be still and know that He is God. My last two years would be woefully different if I didn't believe that to be true.

I am so glad that I will have the privilege of being part of a community of love over the next few days to Eugene and his family, to Jason and Kirstin and their families. I am so glad that they have already felt supported in a plethora of ways I suspect; both big and small. The challenge will be in maintaining consistency of support when the rest of the world will carry on.

To my two grandmother friends and all other grandparents out there, especially those who have experienced the death of a grandchild: My joy as a Nana times four is inexplicable at times. We are honoured to be given the role of grandparents. I *cannot* imagine what it would be like to lose one of my grandbabies. My heart is heavy for my friends. Wisely, someone figured out the harsh reality that grandparents grieve twice over the death of their grandchild; for that precious little lamb who is no longer here and for their parent children. How do they best support those young parents when their hearts are also breaking? Love always wins, so I am prayerful and confident it will rise to the surface here as well.

Perhaps Rick's death is beginning to make a bit more sense to me two years later. It is not difficult for me to reach out when death visits someone else. No, it's not paying it forward; it is not returning the favour per se; it's a whole lot about simply loving another human being when they are knocked down. In this increasingly fast-paced world where many rule their lives by I Phones, Blackberrys or day timers, community gets sacrificed. Maybe that is why I have chosen not to upgrade my dinosaur cell phone or to be ruled by my calendar which could make me sound so important. I choose community and pausing.

Blessings to sweet baby Coby James, his parents and his grandparents.

Chapter 7

We are Family

In the palliative training I provide, we spend one evening determining who constitutes family for the clients our volunteers will visit. In the twenty-first century, 'family is as family does' isn't what it used to be. Biologically, we have all grown up in a family of origin. Today more than ever, blended families, single parents, families with devastating dynamics and those 'intact' families all have a different definition of their family. Family of choice and its fuller definition has expanded to include pets, good friends, church folk, and a host of other people considered significant. My family begins with my sons, daughters-in-law, grandchildren, siblings and extended family. But along the way I/we included Marjorie, Nanoo, Mickdog, our church family and several others.

Even amidst my abundant families of origin and choice, a conundrum with which I wrestle daily is the potential for self-pity. What is the difference between allowing oneself to truly experience the many facets of grief and mourning, and falling into the pit of 'woe is me', helplessness and despair? In her book *The Year of Magical Thinking*, Joan Didion approaches self-pity in a way that really resonates. "The very language we use when we think about self-pity betrays the deep abhorrence in which we hold it; self-pity is feeling sorry for yourself, self-pity is the condition in which those feeling sorry for themselves indulge, or even wallow. Self-pity remains both the most common and the most universally reviled of our character defects, its pestilential destructiveness accepted as given … We are repeatedly left, in other words, with no further focus than ourselves, a source from which self-pity naturally flows. Each time this happens (it happens still) I am struck again by the permanent impassibility of the divide." *Amen, Joan!*

Whether or not I have succumbed to greater degrees of self-pity or simple, unadulterated grief, a mystery for me was the intense physical response I had over the first fifteen months. It was getting ridiculous enough to me that I was reporting less to my kids about different illness situations out of concern that I be seen as 'losing it', seeking attention and pity. Increased anxiety, a panic attack at the beginning of what should have been a most restful time at the lake, vertigo, a couple of urinary tract infections, and passing out at a most public function were part of the exhaustion and re-stabilizing I had *never* anticipated. When I finally divulged more of this ongoing embarrassing 'drama' as I perceived it to my kids, my son Brian responded with this email:

"Mom, I know you have your support network; I just don't want you to feel like you need to hide things from us. We obviously don't judge you for being sick. Shanna said when she was pregnant that she was glad for the sick feelings, because that assured her the baby was growing well. You had the discussion with your replacement GP a while ago that being sick and the frequency and consistency of it was a response to your grief and missing Dad. If this is still a response to the grief, it tells me that you still deeply miss and yearn for your husband and are still daily affected by his absence. To me that is a measure of how deeply you loved each other and depended on each other. It reflects how deeply committed to and all-in you were in your relationship. I know the relationships between spouses and between father and sons are very different, but I often reflect with guilt and regret how infrequently I think about Dad these days, or miss him, or even in some cases remember him. Not that I forget, but it tells me that in my current relationships, I want to be more all-in and committed, to fully know and to be fully known. I don't wish for your physical manifestation of that to continue, nor do I wish you to live out your days wrapped in grief, but I do want you to know that we are your sons, your family, and that we care for you and love you unconditionally. We can't come down and hold your hair back while you puke or wipe your bum (save that for the nursing home), but we can pray and direct thoughts your way and love you from afar."

Terral's response to this email: "I was right with you until the last sentence." *Gotta love my boys!*

A couple of stumbling blocks that my family, friends and I discovered were these. They too loved Rick and for a while my grief was so all consuming I regret now that I did not even see what his sudden death meant to them. In my care giving nature, I didn't want it to be about me, but it was about me. Finding the energy to look outside myself to acknowledge their grief has been most sporadic. To family and friends, I am sorry when I haven't allowed for your grief.

My sons Brian, Terral and I were maybe protecting each other at times, not sharing what was truly in our hearts. Perhaps more now though than initially they are comfortable to call when they have had a memory or one of those moments.

And I have tried to do the same but often I have stopped myself when I think about their busy lives, each with two little children, wonderful wives, jobs, church, maintaining their own homes and their lives. And yet for years we have talked in our groups about the value of family sharing their grief, even when it is difficult to do. Hmmm . . .

However, there have been moments shared by both my boys. A couple of months after Rick died I was having a sleep over at my younger son Terral's. Laura was upstairs bathing the children I believe, I was sweeping their kitchen floor and Terral was putting things away. Prior to my visit, I had asked a friend with marvellous photography skills to use his magic and create a particular photo for me. I had recently had a picture taken of me on the living room couch with four grandbabies surrounding me and it turned out beautifully. In an effort to keep their Papa's memory alive, I asked my friend to Photoshop a lightened head shot of Rick just above the five of us sitting on the couch. It worked perfectly so I had had three 8.5 by 11 copies made; one for me and one each for Brian and Terral.

As Terral and I were finishing up in the kitchen he said to me from behind, "Mum, I don't know about that picture you gave us with Dad in it."

"Okay," I said.

"It feels like you are trying to force Dad to still be with us," Terral blurted out. To which I replied that I had probably done that more for me because I was so missing Rick enjoying his grandbabies. I turned around to find tears streaming down my son's face and we just naturally fell into each other's arms for solace.

About a year after Rick's death, I came home to a message from Brian. Very shortly after that he called again and asked where I had been. There was almost a disgruntled tone to his question. But it became apparent that he was excited about something and he really wanted to tell me about it. Brian is a Music Therapist, which is the perfect vocation for this musically talented, intuitive and sensitive young man. For the first few years of his work, he has worked mostly with elderly people in long-term care settings. He had been working on an in-house concert with his clients and they had presented their program that day. One gentleman with whom Brian's one-to-one interaction had been a bit intermittent showed up for the concert. This man, who had once been an executive for a company, was now in the early stages of dementia. He seemed to be hovering at the front while Brian was getting folks into place so Brian said something like, "It feels like you might have something you want to say, Bill, would you like to?" and handed the gentleman the microphone.

"All right, people," Bill said, "come take your seats, we are about to start and I would like to introduce you to our director Rick McBay." Even though Brian had his nametag on stating his name was Brian McBay, this man called him Rick McBay. No wonder my son wanted to talk to me. We wondered together over the phone what that was all about. Could this man have known Rick in some capacity years ago, or was there another Rick McBay out there? Whatever it was, Brian was quite excited and we just continued to ponder together why that happened.

Secondly, there is much of this grief work (a term coined by Sigmund Freud I believe), that is very much a solo flight. It was and continues to be extremely difficult for me to find words for my friends to understand. At the risk of being cold or dismissive, at times all I can say is, "I'm sorry, but until you are where I am, you can't completely understand." This was a barrier I did not wish to be there but I felt had been created. However, there were also times, when the really raw grief grabbed hold, that maybe it was better to be on one's own. It ain't pretty and too often those we might turn to feel the need to fix instead of just listen and be.

In preparation for returning to my facilitating role in our bereavement support program and an effort towards self-preservation, I sought out a counsellor with whom I visited for five months. Our initial challenge was intriguing in that I had recommended a few people to her over the years and she recommended some to the bereavement program. I recall her handling my initial posturing well and allowing me to get to a place that was real, safe and productive. Perhaps my biggest personal struggle to date has been not getting sucked into the vortex of expectation, comparison and at least some people's perceptions that because I do this work, this should be easier for me. I have been reminded often to take care of myself and give myself permission to work through this the way I need to. It seems it has been a lot easier for me to give that counsel than receive it. The term "giving oneself permission" feels far too overused. We say we should give loved one's permission to die, the survivor's permission to grieve, or permission to take care of one's self. Maybe it's because I have been hearing that expression in those contexts for so long that the words have for me become impotent.

Again, I don't know where the line in the sand is drawn between caring for me and succumbing to self-pity. I guess when I hear women at least, describe that it took them anywhere from two to seven years to feel something close to normal after their husbands died, I can somewhat confidently give myself a break.

Being a person of faith, I consider myself one of the lucky ones whose faith has not faltered. While I am not much of a believer in luck, I don't know other than God's faithfulness to me how else to name that. I have the most wonderful minister in Noel. This young, forty-something man has learned more in his life span than three of mine. He is a voracious learner and is unabashed in sharing his knowledge from the pulpit most energetically, enthusiastically and with humble awe. His command of the Greek language to help us understand what God intended through the Bible is impressive. Plus, Noel 'gets life'. His tears in the hospital with us the night Rick died, his public tears at the funeral and his ability to experience absolute joy with even the smallest of things is delightfully real. Noel has reminded me often what God wants me to know. I am in the centre of God's best plan for me, His outcomes for me are guaranteed because He is faithful. When I am not sure sometimes where God is (although I am sure He is always somewhere) Noel reminds me that God is at work in me, in my pain and He isn't finished yet. In its simplicity, what else do I need to know?

The examples of my evolving family are plentiful. From the neighbour down the road I had not met until a year later that has ensured two years in a row that I receive flowers on December 11, to Amy at Great Lakes, or my sons checking in with their Momma on a regular basis and everyone in between, my family has grown and I am thankful.

Chapter 8

John Richard McBay

Rick's baby pictures reveal a toddler with 'to die for' soft, curly hair and a delightfully impish smile. The youngest of four to Howard and Mary McBay, his siblings would say he got away with much. I don't know when Mary began calling him Ricky, but it stuck, evolving over the years to Ricky Bear, then Rick Bear between him and me.

Growing up next door to his Uncle Lloyd's farm, Rick learned the value of a hard day's work and boasted often of driving a tractor by the age of seven. He learned a lot from farm days with his uncle that he passionately passed on to our boys. Being the youngest, as am I, perhaps the more relaxed approach to child rearing that comes with subsequent children helped Rick learn not to take himself too seriously. And yet that work ethic learned at a young age to do any job completely and with pride propelled him. As Terral insisted be included in his father's death announcement: "You do it big, huge and fantastic, and you do it right . . ."

Rick would be the first to say that academia was not his strong suit through the elementary and high school years. In fact, he was quick to admit that he liked Grade 12 so well, he did it a second time. His greatest source of pride in elementary school was being involved in the time capsule placed in a cornerstone of the then brand new Anna Melick Public school in Dunnville, Ontario. He was in Grade 7 or 8 at the time and I still have the photo of that 'historic' day.

As his Great Lakes Christian High School students would learn some forty years later, Rick discovered that not all important learning happened in the classroom. He was a hands on kind of guy but he also read voraciously. Every single issue of Readers' Digest and Maclean's magazine were read from front to back cover. Sometimes that would drive me crazy because I was a talker; perhaps that is why he read so much. Often our much coveted Saturday morning coffees together would not be complete without him putting down his Maclean's magazine and impishly stating, "I guess we should talk about the relationship now." I miss him now in his chair by the window, devouring whatever he could read to remain current in the world.

Rick took his teaching job very seriously. While he was the only teacher at Great Lakes who did not have his official teaching diploma (and not having that piece of paper sadly branded him somewhat), he was awesome at this work he saw as a privilege. It was not unusual for the otherwise quiet Mr. McBay to get rather animated sometimes in the classroom and pull a *Dead Poet's Society* antic of standing on a desk to motivate his students or stress a point. Probably his greatest teaching abilities were in Music and History, both sources of passion. Many students' comments in the wall mural and memory book created at the school when he died echoed a similar theme: "Mr. McBay didn't teach me how to sing as much as he taught me I 'could' sing." OR: "I learned more from Mr. McBay outside the classroom, on stage, during chorus or on field trips to the War Plane Museum."

Probably the most telling words of Rick's positive influence with his students come from Matthew's entry in the memory book:

"Mr. McBay, I love you and miss you. I regret never letting you know how much I really appreciated you. I always looked forward to working with you and in the same way, look forward to seeing you again. Whenever I worked with you I could expect to learn a multitude of new things. And I don't know if I ever conveyed how much I love that. I could ask you anything, you were always looking to teach me something, whether it was gently pointing the right way to do something or throwing tools at me until I got it right. You taught me more outside the classroom than inside and you taught me even more when you didn't say anything at all. You were the example for me, but most of all you were my friend, and a fantastic one at that. I can't say how hard it is for me to let go, so I won't. I will miss working with you backstage, and during the summer. I can't say how much this hurts, to make a deal with you and never even be able to fulfil it now that you're not here. My life would not be what it is without your guidance, and encouragement. You've taught me how to serve and how to do it right. You've taught me how to live and how to do it best. Love Matt."

Becoming a Queen Scout in his teens along with his brother Gary was a very big source of pride for Rick. Scouting provided a whole different source of education, again, none of which happened in the classroom. I now wear his Queen Scout ring and gave Gary Rick's Queen Scout cuff-links this past summer for his seventieth birthday. Judging by some of the jesting comments from my nephews, I am not sure they were convinced of the value of Scouting. I find that sad because it would appear they are not alone as is supported by the statistical decline in Scouting over the years. Sorry Baden Powell, but you've got to know that your program's vision for young boys and men was an exciting adventure for this man.

> In son Brian's gift of love to his father at his funeral, he lamented that Rick was just getting into his 'Papahood' and now he is gone. Again, not knowing exactly what Rick now experiences in heaven, this may also be one of my greatest laments. Carter and Leah especially were getting to the age where going exploring with Papa in our yard and to the back creek was becoming a pretty cool thing to do. Campfires, planting the garden, raking leaves, discovering bugs, rides in the wheelbarrow or on the tractor were all very fun things to do together. Haley enjoyed it too but she also liked just having Papa hold her and that bonding touch was precious to both of them. At four months of age, Seth would only know and remember Papa through photos. There was just so much more to do together as Papa and grandchildren. Fortunately, my four munchkins will continue to see at least a bit of their Papa through their dads.

Rick's love for me was deep, faithful and unconditional. He was incredibly patient and put up with me being a bit of a spoiled brat sometimes. Romance was not always his strong suit and yet he took my breath away on occasion. However, more predictably, and I am not speaking ill of the dead, Rick's idea of a date was going out for supper on a Friday night, usually my idea, then heading to Home Depot or Canadian Tire.

But for our tenth anniversary, a time when we were struggling in our marriage, he bought me the emerald and diamond engagement ring he could not afford when we decided to marry. I was also going through some rebellious thing at that time where I regarded engagement rings with disdain; seeing them as lame, materialistic expressions of love. Ah the sixties. Speaking of lame!

One Christmas, a year or so after my parents and his mother had died, we went a little overboard with presents, compensating our boys, we thought, for the grandparents they never really got to enjoy and be spoiled by. Our living room was a sea of wrapping paper but Rick declared there was one more gift. He and the boys disappeared outside for a couple of minutes and returned struggling through the back door with something big covered by a blanket. Underneath the blanket was the completely restored cedar chest my father had bought my mother for a wedding gift in 1942, the original bill of sale still inside. But what was most spectacular about this gift was what was required to restore it. When I was a teenager, my mother decided to redecorate my bedroom, which involved some pretty wild orange and yellow striped wallpaper (this was the sixties after all). She had a lot of wallpaper left over and one did not waste, so she had the bright idea of completely covering that beautiful cedar chest with the paper and several layers of lacquer on top. Years later, that beastly box sat in our garage collecting multiple layers of dust until this well-planned act of love, and to this day I cannot fathom how or where Rick took the hours upon hours to restore this treasure. I cried like a baby when I saw it.

Being a Dad came naturally to Rick. Although both of us were rather nervous bringing our first born Brian home from the hospital, we rather hysterically got the hang of things pretty quickly after our first diaper change in his freshly painted and papered nursery. Brian peed all over both of us and we laughed ourselves silly, concluding that somehow we were going to be fine. Terral was quite literally our Christmas baby, born at 1:22 Christmas morning 1981, which has lent to the meaning of our Christmas in a most special way. We all loved Christmas at our house, especially late at night when all but the tree lights were turned off allowing for peaceful, magical moments in the quiet as a family or as a couple.

Rick made sure he taught as much of the practical stuff as he could to Brian and Terral. He took them on long bike rides when they were still small enough to ride in his back carrier. He took them camping, played hours of catch with them on the side lawn, versed them in all things to do with excellent sound production and passed on the enthusiasm for good music, campfires, gardening, composting and making maple syrup in our back yard.

Having a relationship with our Creator God was a given for Rick. I don't recall a time he ever experienced doubt unless he hid it very well, which I doubt. A number of influences along the way contributed to a steely yet ever searching faith in a God he knew loved him. Parents Mary and Howard made sure all four of their kids grew up in the United Church. Mary was a piano teacher and taught music in the Dunnville elementary schools. All four children had to complete Grade 8 piano, so music was one way of learning about God through the great Masters, through hymns sung on Sunday mornings and the choir experience.

Greater education became much more inviting, palatable and necessary to Rick after we were married. Before we met, he and a friend partnered and created a successful sound production business in every way except monetarily. Mobius Audio offered some wonderful opportunities for Rick to mix and produce really good concert sound for several established or up and coming artists in the late sixties and early seventies. Concerts with B.B. King, Chuck Mangione, Anne Murray, Van Morrison, Lighthouse, Crowbar, Ike and Tina Turner, to name a few, were exciting times. And I love to boast about that for Rick. Get him started on Tina Turner and you would be guaranteed hearing about her legs! We discovered shortly after we met that Rick had produced the sound for Chuck Mangione at the same concert in Massey Hall that I attended the summer of 1971. Chuck was at the height of his career at that time and little did we know we were both fans of his music.

Other jobs, most of them working with challenged teens in residential programs, led him to conclude that there was something else out there for him to do that was important and teaching became his focus. While working full time at Robert Land Academy, Rick attended Brock University towards a double major in Music and Religious Studies. Brian and Terral were young; more than a few times we all lamented how much work and school took Daddy away from us, but in two long years at this pace Rick graduated with distinction from a degree that most would have taken three years to complete. When I think of that time, I honestly don't know how we all came out intact. But our pride was quite visible the day of his graduation when two little boys held a 'Congratulations, Daddy, we love you' banner in the aisle as he proceeded by us with hundreds of other graduates.

Out of that time came a greater confidence and peace for Rick around his belief that God, His son Jesus and the Holy Spirit truly do exist. Right around that time also, we made a very significant change in our church affiliation. I had grown up in the Anglican Church then joined Rick in the united faith upon marriage. But as our boys grew, a growing concern for their biblical teaching as well as our own directed us to seek out other faith communities where we knew the Bible was at the centre.

The Church of Christ was introduced to us and we were immediately immersed in what we felt strongly was solid teaching as well as a most caring church community. The challenge for us both having been raised with music, was in the fact that this particular faith community did not use any musical instruments in their worship of God. While originally very odd to both of us and part of an inherited doctrine we never embraced as an ingredient to our salvation, we jumped in with both feet. We liked the idea that this church community was autonomous in its decision making, was shepherded by elders and a minister, that we weren't going through the motions each week of a common prayer book, and that many lay people contributed to the corporate worship each week. We grew to enjoy the a cappella singing and with Rick's musical abilities, he worked very hard to make our singing more glorious to God's ears and our own. If we are going to sing without an instrument, then we better sing well. This passion for Rick led us to several a cappella workshops in the States and each time we brought back new, more contemporary hymns home to Canada to share. But we also brought with us the need to have a healthy respect for the old and new and I believe we can boast in our church family of thirty years now that a wonderful blend of both 'How Great Thou Art' and 'From the Inside Out' or the like can be expected each time we gather for corporate worship. Rick got the fact that faith and worship are very personal, very individual, sometimes very spontaneous and worthy of our attention to detail.

While travelling was something we both really enjoyed, I noticed the last couple of years before Rick died his increasing hesitance to explore bigger trip ideas. I had begun plans to take him to Europe and visit places like Normandy, Vimy Ridge and Barth Germany where my father's POW Concentration Camp once stood. The two World Wars about which Rick taught his students bore tremendous meaning for him and his appreciation for life, justice and humanity. But travelling that far and for a time worthy of the expense did not carry the same excitement it did for me.

There were other little things that I have reflected upon in retrospect that tell me now that perhaps something was amuck of which we had no idea. Rick got cold very easily, he could like his father, nap at the drop of a hat, and the energizer bunny energy had been replaced with a much milder version. Perhaps the most astonishing thing was Rick starting to say "no" a little more occasionally because he was seeing and feeling the need to pause and 'be'. Most certainly, our last ten years of marriage were indeed the best. Rick didn't get to do all the things on his bucket list, we didn't get to go to Alaska together and he didn't get to enjoy all the hard earned privileges of retirement and spending more time with his grandchildren. I will always be sad about that but I am counting on where he is now to be positively extraordinary by comparison.

Chapter 9

The Story of Us

Twelve weeks after Rick died and there was much to say around the experience; navigating through the fog, celebrating and now grieving the surprising but diminishing felt support I was aware would happen. After the last sympathy card arrived, the phone calls and social invitations were less, a reality that saddened me at times. *That sounds rather pitiful doesn't it?* So, let me also say that along the way there have been many wonderful surprises, which would unfold with the need to tell this story.

Rick and I met one summer evening in 1973 at a camp where I was counselling, the first of its kind in Canada for children with learning disabilities. Its director, my neighbour I grew up with in Oakville, bought an old farm in the country which would, with our fledgling farmers' help, become a residential camp complete with tent platforms, water stations and more all in the woods.

We were building kybos that night (outdoor toilets for those never having the privilege of attending summer camp). I was wielding a pretty mean circular saw, cutting the sides for three kybos when our camp cook introduced us to her cousin Rick, a guy who had been involved in Scouting forever and liked working with kids. She had told him about this unique camp program and he wanted to see it for himself. For thirty-seven years after that night, Rick loved to remind me, usually in the company of others, that I was a tough choice out of three girls he thought would be cool to ask out for a date. Funny, he never did ask the other two. We were married two years later. I recall having great difficulty at that post-sixties time in my life getting my head around the biblical assertion of what God desired for the marriage relationship in that we two should become one. My naivety and rebellious spirit at the time sparked great inner concern that my individuality would be sacrificed completely. I was wrong.

We bought our first home three years after that and started our family with the birth of Brian in 1978, followed by Terral on Christmas Day, 1981.

Because both of us had experience before marriage working with kids from troubled homes or boys' institutions, Rick and I were pretty sure we had all the answers regarding raising children. A very dear and wise friend named Eleanor, who quickly became Nanoo when a much younger son Brian could not pronounce her name, gently and lovingly warned us about our over assuredness (some would say we were down right cocky). Over the years her wisdom regularly re-visited us, but I would like to think that over all we did some things right and after our sons married wonderful women and began their own families, we couldn't be more proud.

Our marriage was by no means perfect. We fought the most and ferociously over money the first decade until I begrudgingly took over the paying of bills. When it came to investments and planning for our future from jobs that would never earn us the big bucks, Rick had a better handle on that while my eyes would glaze over during any discussions with our financial advisor.

We were forced to face a couple of very difficult situations in our life involving poor choices, one of which threatened our marriage significantly. Had we not sought out a church family ten years before, which proved to be pivotal in both our faith walks, I am not sure we would have hung in there.

Rick's father died six months before we were married at the age of sixty-three. I didn't really understand at the time what that was like for him. My parents and his mother died over a two-year period at the end of the eighties. Being orphaned was something we then could share. As a young woman whose grandparents all died before she had turned seven years of age, and who years later saw her boys suffer a similar lack of one of life's most important relationships, I had vowed I would be around for our grandchildren. There is simply no other relationship that is as unique and joyful as grand parenting. All of our friends had grandchildren at least seven or eight years before Rick and I; their falling over themselves to tell us the latest miraculous thing their grandchild had done was at times almost annoying. While I am now not guilty of gushing over others with stories of my grandbabies, I am definitely a convert and celebrate my Nana status with pride and the ferocity of a mother lion.

Unemployment thrust upon Rick in 1992 tested our family significantly for the next couple of years. It still hurts a bit now to recall some of the comments and judgement said behind his back or sometimes directly. To continue putting food on the table and pay bills, Rick always found work, some jobs many would turn up their noses at. I allowed myself briefly to be waivered by the judgement of others and was not as supportive as I could have been. Short lived thankfully but I can never erase that lack of belief in him. The upside was Rick applying for and securing the position of Director of the Hamilton Male Police Chorus, even if it was just part time. I don't know if those men will ever comprehend what his seventeen-year relationship with them did for his ego. Once Rick began teaching full time at Great Lakes Christian High School, he was exactly where he wanted and needed to be in his life.

We were fortunate enough to travel a bit over our thirty years together; to the Bahamas a couple of times, Hawaii when we were pregnant with Terral, and to several United States. Taking our boys to Disneyworld at the ages of ten and seven was perfect timing and a two-week trip to the west coast a couple of years later as a family of four fostered some wonderful family memories. In 2007, our last big trip together as a couple was to explore the east coast of Canada over a three-week period. Rick boasted often that we were able to have lunch every day somewhere by the sea and we vowed we would return the summer of 2011. While the majesty of the BC Mountains was glorious and unforgettable, the east coast with its more down home pace, delightful people, seafood and ceilidhs struck a chord in both of us.

Three times we made the trek to Lancaster PA to take in some spectacular Biblical musicals at the world famous Sight and Sound Theatre. Bringing to life the stories of *Ruth, In the Beginning* and the *Psalms of David* with top notch young actors, animals and birds accentuating the authenticity of the times, was faith affirming as well as most entertaining. Lancaster is in the middle of Amish country and can take you into a world we have all but forgotten, but in which many faithful people inhabit. Our respect for the life the Amish have chosen to live and protect increased with each visit.

The Bed and Breakfast we stayed in, which was situated at the edge of a large Amish farm, provided a wonderful backdrop for us with friends to sit in the moonlight after a wonderful day. We were easily entranced by the clip clop of the horses as they drew their buggies of families back to their homes in the countryside we had marvelled at during the day. Perhaps Rick's most favourite activity the one year was attending a good old-fashioned Steam Show in a neighbouring county of Lancaster. You know the expression, "happier than a pig in poop?" Having grown up working on his Uncle Lloyd's farm, Rick learned much about the land and how farm equipment "in the old days" operated. I have shared with a few people a little steam engine he acquired in his teens. When Rick first showed me with absolute joy how this little engine worked I looked at him rather perplexed and asked, "What exactly is the point?" Not my finest hour. Fortunately, he was able to pass along some of that awe and knowledge to our sons.

When we were both growing up, music was an integral part of our life learning and became a part of our souls. Personally, I am not sure there is another language on the planet that is as universal and has the potential to grab us at our very core. Rick's musical ability excelled far beyond my own and I am okay with that. In our a cappella singing group, leading singing at church or directing the Hamilton Male Police Chorus, he had the uncanny and annoying ability to identify any note from any part sung incorrectly. Fortunately for all, Rick was very gracious about pointing out the error of our ways, but I always marvelled at that ability which has been most naturally inherited by both Brian and Terral. Brian is an accredited Music Therapist and Terral leads worship at his church with his voice and guitar or percussion accompaniment. Each time I hear my sons sing, I fall in love all over again.

So as a family, we did much together musically. There were a few fundraising concerts for our Great Lakes Christian High School over the years in which all four McBays sang together. Both Brian and Terral's weddings incorporated wonderful music, and as my minister Noel said at the beginning of Rick's funeral on December 16, 2010: "We are *so* going to sing today." Most gloriously, the near 700 people in attendance were practically drawn to their knees when eighty plus Great Lakes chorus students past and present stood up to sing *The Greatest Commands* in a cappella four part harmony. Rick was honoured and God was indeed glorified.

There is so much more to the story of us but I will conclude this portion with reflective words written a couple of months after Rick died, "What Do I Miss?"

As I am still not sure how exactly to find my way through this most uninvited life passage, this will need to be an ongoing document. And while I am already tiring of "I'm sorry for your loss" or "you will need to go through all the firsts of the next year without Rick", that will be a part of this ongoing experience.

Son Brian and I had been lamenting an almost complete lack of feeling six weeks later over the fact that his Dad, my husband, had died. While neither of us wanted to prescribe to or manufacture emotional responses, *we wanted to feel something!*

So, I started a list of all the things I was missing about Rick. And I encouraged a few of my female friends to consider writing similar lists about their husbands with whom they are still blessed to have a presence. Just in case I am guilty of putting him on a pedestal as a somewhat twisted way to remember him, Rick was not a saint and we spent thirty-five years of marriage finding ways around each other's foibles, but we did indeed come to a place of comfort and peace. And while I know for everything there is a time and season, it will feel to me for the rest of my life that Rick Bear, Papa died way too soon.

"What do I miss?"

I miss the warming presence of Rick beside me in bed, and find hugging his Great Lakes fleece jacket a weak substitute.

I miss his ridiculously comical 'bucksnorts' first thing in the mornings as he is making coffee and not quite able to complete the task before heading to the loo.

I miss him looking at me with a silly grin and saying, "I love you, Sandy," when I have said something funny.

I miss the incredible tenderness that practically oozed out of him when around his grandbabies and his fascination for their moments of discovery.

I miss the fact that he won't see Haley's little boot prints in the snow, or hear Carter or Leah say, "I yuv you, Papa."

I miss that he barely got to know baby Seth.

I miss his most annoying (not really), "Fifty bucks please," with hand out-stretched whenever he made any kind of house repair, or his, "Let me just go to my storage shed of useful things and see if I can't fix that."

I miss his being happiest in our living room over Saturday morning coffee, something that would literally get him through each busy week.

I miss his absolute bliss during sap time or playing in his compost heaps.

I miss his creative Christmas gifts and the fact that sometimes he would buy something months ahead and then tell me he had. Apparently, there is a gift for me right now, somewhere in our home.

I miss him putting down his Maclean's magazine (which he read faith-fully from cover to cover each week) and saying, "I suppose we need to talk about the relationship now."

I miss the fact that he was willing to talk about the relationship and listen when I needed to vent.

I miss our conversations about his students and how he could better reach them with some times unconventional but most creative ways.

I miss our conversations about our kids, grandbabies and how we can best support without being seen as interfering.

I will miss our plans to go back out east this summer.

I will miss our plans to go to Alaska and together, take our family to Disneyworld when the grandbabies would have been old enough to enjoy it.

I will miss Rick, Brian, Terral, and now Carter and Seth being able to play catch on the side lawn.

I will miss campfires late at night or sitting on the swing, sometimes with a glass of wine.

I will miss our regular Friday night 'dates' going to Canadian Tire and out for supper.

I will miss as Brian described Rick's 'Wikipedia' volumes of knowledge and wisdom.

I am missing and will continue to miss Rick's presence at home, in the yard, at church, at Great Lakes and at the cottage.

I will miss being able to finish each other's sentences or look at each other with a knowing nod when our kids or grandbabies do some-thing awesome.

"I miss my husband Rick a whole lot . . ."

Regardless of what I might understand and believe about what Rick is experiencing in heaven, a deep sadness besets us all when Carter, Leah, Haley or Seth accomplish something new, charm us, or in the wisdom only children have, ask the big questions about Papa. As son Brian said at the funeral, "Papa was just getting into his prime of 'Papahood' and now he is gone." Deep emotion is felt when those wonderful little people do or say something to knock us off our feet. *Rick, did you see/hear that?*

Terral sent an email recently about a conversation he and three-year-old Leah had while he was working on his basement renovation. At three years of age she was processing how family works. Terral wrote: "Leah regularly reminds me that you're my mommy and Papa was my daddy, and that I, her father, miss my daddy. I told her I do miss my daddy. She helped me put up the two new lights in the basement. I asked her if she knew where I learned how to do that. She said she didn't know. I told her Papa taught me. She asked 'why?' Ha! I told her Papa and I liked working on things together so it's nice to be able to remember Papa when we fix things because he's the one who taught me how. I think she started to trail off around this point, but it is cool to still talk about Dad with her."

Carter being the oldest grandchild was the one who talked most about Papa. However, both Leah and Haley had asked more than once why Papa can't get better and come back to us. Death is still pretty abstract for all of my grandchildren, but it is wonderful that they continue to think of him in their own precious ways.

A note to married couples – July 23, 2013 . . .

This past several months, a number of regrets from our 35.5 years of marriage have raised their ugly little heads in my consciousness. They are very difficult to remember and reconcile but I am working on it. To those of you who have begun to take each other for granted, GET OVER YOURSELVES AND STOP IT! None of us can take back hurtful things and saying I'm sorry more than being proactive before we speak just doesn't cut it. Remember why you fell in love. Work to restoring some of that magic and show each other regularly that the love is still there, ever changing, ever strengthening. Hold hands, go for walks, get your heads out of technology and talk with each other face to face. I want to shake people silly when I see or hear them being derogatory or disrespectful with each other. YOU CAN'T TAKE THAT BACK AND YOU MAY NOT GET A SECOND CHANCE. If you are both looking to each other's best interests instead of your own, guess what? You are both being loved and LOVE ALWAYS WINS.

And that's all I have to say about that

. . .

Chapter 10

Grief Shared, Grief Understood

Because no two reactions to grief will ever be the same, it is important to look at how others have responded to the death of a loved one. To that end, I invited friends and people within our bereavement program to share their experience. They were given a few questions to help them get started. Some responded only to the questions, others wove them into a story. The telling of their stories will underline, I hope, the need for those witnessing or supporting to understand there is no cookie cutter approach to grief or the support they will hopefully endeavour to offer.

Ev and Iris share what their lives are like without their husbands. Anne willingly shares her grief after the death of my Uncle Don. Laurena, Pat and my son Brian offer their thoughts on the death of their parent. Kirstin writes about life without her newborn son, and her mother Elisabeth who I fondly call Elsje, tells us the double grief from a grandmother's heart.

From Ev – In memory of Don

I have known Ev for more than fifteen years. Upon retirement, she and her husband Don had moved to the area and Ev sought out Rose Cottage Visiting Volunteers to become a palliative volunteer. Her interest in becoming a facilitator with the bereavement support program was sparked and we have grown in our friendship since.

Ev's husband Don, who I liked very much, died in 2008. I recall the day, September 27. When I heard he had died, I called their home and left a rather pitiful, teary voice message which caused her daughter some alarm: "This is the Sandy you do bereavement work with Mum?!" Clearly my message didn't instill confidence.

When Ev sent me her response to this request she told me she did not include Don's name because for her that was too personal.

"I can't say when I knew he wasn't going to get well, there had been several instances: Encephalitis, seizures, suspected heart problems, a lump on his thyroid that had to be removed, kidney and liver problems, all this and more over a three-year period. We both talked positively about this last bout of seizures, they would pass and he would be okay again. But one day I knew this was not going to be the case, and since some dementia was also happening, I don't think he realized how ill he was.

"Immediately following his death, everyone was there to continue the support we had been receiving for the past three years. Family, friends, work colleagues, neighbours, etc. However, while my family had continued to be supportive, I believe my friends expected me not to want to talk about him so they acted as though he wasn't really dead and not coming back.

"We were a couple; that of course has changed. While my friends certainly tried to include me in events, it wasn't them (although I used to think it was), it was me who was different and felt the odd one out. I felt that way for at least two years. In the third year I started to create a new life for myself, nothing dramatic but while beginning to enjoy our friends again, I also enjoyed doing things by myself and creating new friendships.

"I would not say my faith has been diminished or changed; my beliefs are just about the same.

What has surprised me is the energy I now feel to create a life for me without him. I still think about him every day and wish things could have been different, but I am able to plan new adventures for myself and enjoy them. Yes, I am moving forward, but still deeply love the man I spent fifty years of my life with and never see that changing."

From Iris - In memory of Bill

I have known Iris as a Rose Cottage Visiting Volunteer and as a member of our Single Rose 'sisterhood'. Iris wrote this nine months after her husband died very suddenly.

"For about three-four weeks prior, Bill had been complaining about soreness in his neck and left shoulder and arm. I kept telling him that he had to contact his cardiologist. But you know men; he kept saying that he must have slept wrong. He did share with our neighbour Ed that he was having trouble breathing one day when he was cutting the grass. His pain was so bad one night that he slept sitting up.

"Bill and I had been out with Jane and Bob, attending the spaghetti dinner fundraiser at their church. Bill had been asking about when it was coming up. We went and had dinner and had a lovely time. Bill was quiet for the most part and I had to engage him in conversation with us. We were to join Jane and Bob at their home afterwards for a visit. Bill wasn't looking very well and so we begged off for another time. He asked me if I would drive home, which was odd. When we got home, we both changed our clothes. I stayed up in our bedroom to do some reading while Bill went downstairs to watch a football game. The next thing I knew, the paramedics were in my room waking me up to say that Bill had dialed 911. I ran downstairs and he was sitting on the sofa. They transported him to West Lincoln Memorial Hospital. He was assessed there before deciding if he should be taken to the Hamilton General Hospital. They stabilized him and suggested that I go home and get some rest. I asked Bill what it was he wanted me to do and he said to go home, get some rest, come back after attending the play on Sunday afternoon. The hospital staff told me that once they had more information or if his condition changed they would call and if I had not heard from them by 7am to call them. I woke up to their call. When I arrived at the hospital I was taken into an examining room where the doctor proceeded to tell me that they did everything possible for him but unfortunately they lost him. I was in shock to say the least. I was expecting to go and see him before they were to take him to Hamilton.

"*Felt areas of support?* I feel lots of support from family and friends.

"Something that has not been helpful is people saying, 'Give me a call if there is anything that I can do to help you get through this.' I have moved on as much as possible. Getting things sorted out at home that were meant to be done before Bill's passing but there never seemed to be time.

"*What have I learned?* How precious and short life can be and is.

Has your faith been diminished or enhanced? Absolutely enhanced.

What has surprised me? How some days I can't stop crying and then other days I move along normally as though he is still at home waiting for me to get in from work and start nagging at him! *Am I moving forward and how do I know?* Some days I feel as though I'm moving forward, friends comment on how well I seem to be doing by moving forward, other days I feel frozen in time.

What do I miss? I miss coming home to Bill sitting on the sofa either reading or watching one of his many favourite TV programs.

"I miss sitting and watching Coronation Street with him. He would say to me when I was going out, 'Oh, but you are going to miss Cory Street.' For most of our marriage he was a stay-at-home person while I 'had' to be out and about doing something that I felt was constructive and not 'wasting time' reading or watching TV, which was one of our issues. But boy, what would I give to have that issue back."

From Anne who loved my Uncle Don (Anderson) very much

"Don took his final breath Thursday morning at 10:30, November 22, 2012 at the Charles Lemoyne Hospital. Jim (Don's son) and I were with him all through the night. I had gone home to pick up my pills. I arrived ten minutes too late. His soul had departed. The room was dark when Jim opened the blinds. Sunshine filled the room and the warm rays of that very sun that Don loved and longed for, embraced him. I held his hand which was still warm and kissed him gently. 'Good bye, my love.' He was my soul mate, my sunshine, my happiness.

"Two weeks have passed and I'm listening to Nat King Cole singing *Autumn Leaves.* '. . . I will miss you most of all when autumn leaves begin to fall.' I knew that one day I would be listening to that song and weep.

"Sitting alone in my living room and watching the sun's rays passing through a little crystal sun catcher that Don gave me, I see diamonds dancing on my carpet and on the walls. It's 10:30 in the morning. *I am not alone!*

"I look around and see an enlarged photo of our galloping Belgian Beauties coming to fetch their favourite treats of apples, carrots, clover and sometimes a cube of sugar which we fed them regularly. These beautiful horses came to know us and never hesitated to greet us and pose for us.

I see another enlargement of two majestic swans dancing together and forming a heart with their necks. I see two chickadees in my hand. I remember that their little feet were warm even on that cold winter day. I see three horses in the mist. I see ornaments, frogs of every size and shape, books on birds and butterflies, horses and cats. Don loved cats and was fond of my little Mimi. I see photo albums filled with memories. I see a picture of Don wearing his favourite cap and tweed jacket. I hear music. *I'm not alone!*"

From Laurena - In memory of Erwin Goossen

Laurena is a surgical nurse, a dear friend who has persistently included me and who is wife to my dear funeral director friend Ralph. This is her story of her father.

August 8, 2008 - The day my Dad graduated to glory

"My 'journey' with Dad actually starts three months earlier in May 2008 when he suffered a small stroke. He became progressively weak, along with some back pain in June and July, which resulted in many doctor appointments and tests. I was able to go with him to all of those visits for which I was very grateful (quality father/daughter time). Dad was always kind, gracious and never questioned or challenged the doctors. I continued to go see him almost every day, (which in hindsight was a precious gift).

"August long weekend was the beginning of the end. He 'enjoyed' a family dinner at my sister's on Saturday night. Sunday morning, I stopped in on my way to church to see him and he was weak and nauseated. After medication and a day of rest he felt marginally better . . . enough to have some watermelon. This would turn out to be one of his last 'favourite food' experiences.

"Monday morning I woke up at 8:00 with a 'feeling' to go see him – I had never gone over there that time of day (God's Hand in it?). My Mom hurried to the door when she saw me cycle onto the driveway. Dad had become weaker and had gone back to bed. He had no complaints of pain or nausea so I let him rest, telling him I would come back later to check on him. At 10:00 he was still resting. His blood pressure was low so

I thought he should go to the emergency. Unable to transport him myself due to his weakened condition, a call was placed to 911. The last leg of the journey was about to begin.

"After numerous phone calls to family members, my Mom and I followed Dad's ambulance to West Lincoln Memorial Hospital (WLMH) emergency. Blood tests, X-rays, ECG and ultrasound were done and results were presented to us very efficiently. The news wasn't great but steps were made to resolve the abnormalities. Low hemoglobin resulted in a blood transfusion making him stronger, heart medications to counteract the abnormal ECG and pain medication to resolve back discomfort. Despite my efforts to transfer him to a bigger health centre, we were informed he did not meet the criteria and would remain at WLMH in a monitored ICU bed.

"All this information was passed on to my family (more than forty). My younger sister and I decided to stay the night. Thankfully he had a good sleep. The following day, Tuesday, our meeting with the doctor was devastating. Dad had an abnormal mass in his pancreas. A CAT scan needed to be done to confirm and determine at what stage 'it' was.

"During this time, numerous family members were milling in and out of the ICU and virtually taking over the entire second floor and waiting room of the hospital. Thank goodness that 'wing' was closed for the week due to holidays. I remember at one point telling my sister, 'This is very precious family time which, when we look back, we will never regret.' To this day that rings true for all of us!

"Late Wednesday evening my sister flew in from B.C. She talked to Dad, and then left with the rest of the family. My sister Carolyn and I settled in for our third night at the 'Hilton waiting room'. Around 1:00 am the nurse came in and told us to come and see Dad right away. After years of giving that same statement to 'waiting room families', I knew all too well what was to come. While Carolyn called the rest of the family, I went in and helped as the team assessed, discussed and performed procedures on Dad. At one point, the doctor had Dad sit up and hug me so he could listen to his lungs. That hug was the best part of my week. Once Dad had stabilized, the rest of the family could come in, technically only two at a time, but in reality, more. We would all stay with him till Friday. Thursday was filled with Dad being able to speak to most of his children and grandchildren with a sweet smile on his face and a gentle hand on their shoulder. We were able to share prayers, tears, singing, memories and laughter. His wonderful grandchildren supplied nourishment. As we took our turns sitting with Dad, pastors, friends and extended family stopped by to offer greatly appreciated comfort. Thursday evening Dad's children and our Mom settled for the night using stretchers, floor mats and chairs as beds.

"Around 4:30 Friday morning, Dad's breathing was becoming more laboured. After the nurses made him more comfortable, Mom and all eight children stood around his bed singing and praying. Mom held Dad's hand and, through tears, recited verses to him.

"At 5:00 am – 08/08/08 – with his eight children around him, my father took his last breath. Well done, thy good and faithful servant! *We love you, Dad!*

"That journey was quite remarkable and I am continuously amazed as I relive the story for all the gifts I received and continue to cherish.

"At the funeral and the weeks, months and years to follow, many people have told me their stories about Dad and how he touched their lives:

"'Your Dad was always there to help us when we worked in the church kitchen.'

"'Your Dad never complained when he had to clean up after a youth function – he would just be glad the youths were at church and not on the streets.'

"'Your Dad would always make sure the gym was ready when our volleyball league needed to use it.'

"'Your Dad did such a great job in leading our Bible study.'

"'We loved singing with your Dad.'

"'Your Dad was always willing to go the second mile.'

"'Your Dad would look after my kids so I could arrange the flowers for Sunday morning.'

"A mother shared with us that when she told her four-year-old child that Mr. Goossen had died, the child had said: 'Oh, you mean Jesus in jeans.' This lovely toddler had thought the man that took 'care' of the church and was always so kind must have been 'Jesus in jeans'.

"'Your Dad made sure the floors were clean for my Pilates class.'

"'We are all going to miss Mr. Goossen.'"

From my son Brian who couldn't wait to tell me about this which he entitled: 'The trombone Incident'.

Brian recounted an experience in a music store that rattled him a bit. While in one of the store aisles, the characteristic sounds of a trombone being played live caused Brian to freeze where he stood. Trombone was his Dad's principal instrument in a brass band as a teen, during his music studies through university and when he taught trombone to his students at Great Lakes. Being a music therapist, Brian 'got' the impact of this emotional moment only too well. Here it is in his words . . .

"My son Carter and I were in the local music store to pick up some equipment for my work as a music therapist. Carter and I and the music store are usually a good combination because I can spend some time looking around at what I want and Carter can busy himself playing the electric drum kits with the headphones on. After the drum kits, we usually head upstairs so I can play one of the baby grand pianos and imagine a day when I'll have one in my own home. Once upstairs, Carter decided he wanted to try playing each of the fifteen ukuleles that were hanging on the wall. As I was retrieving another one for him to play, someone on the other side of the store began playing the trombone. The sound of that instrument stopped me in my tracks, and was the strongest association with Dad that I've had since he died.

"The funny thing about that is I only remember a handful of times I actually heard Dad play the trombone. I remember him playing the Superman Theme song once or twice at a church party on New Year's Eve. More recently, I remember him playing Christmas carols on the trombone while I accompanied on the piano, and him playing as part of the band program at the high school where he taught music. When I take a moment to think about Dad and remember him, the trombone does come up as something I associate with him, but it's definitely not at the top of the list. But when I heard that trombone playing in the store that day, the first and only thing I thought of was Dad. I felt goose bumps on my arms, I stopped what I was doing with Carter; I stood still and listened. I won't say that I expected to turn around and see him there playing, but in my mind's eye, it was him. The tone and clarity were excellent, just like his was.

"The proximity of the sound also played a part in the association. I've heard the trombone played on a CD since Dad died, but never had the same response as I did when I heard it live in the same room as me. So, when I turned around and saw the player, a young man with shaggy hair underneath a woolen toque, and an equally shaggy beard, playing a vivid blue trombone . . . well, needless to say, the aura of the moment was shattered. And not in a bad way. I remember laughing to myself at how unexpected it was for me to see who I saw, when I was picturing and remembering someone totally different. While it was a bit painful, in that it brought back such strong memories of him with such force (a rare thing for me, two years after his death), it was mostly a wonderful experience, and a welcome opportunity to remember him. I find myself thankful that I do still remember him, miss him, and that two years of absence hasn't at all erased thirty-two years of relationship."

From Pat – In memory of her mother Marj MacKinnon

Pat and I grew up together from the age of seven or eight years of age. We attended elementary and high school together and shared closely in each other's lives for close to twenty five years. Having tea at her place after school, often with Marj, was a part of our upbringing.

"My Mom Marjorie moved on to heaven March 28, 2012 at 6:45 am. Mom had been acutely ill with a GI bug a few weeks before and was hospitalized for dehydration, given antibiotics preventatively and ended up contracting a 'super bug', C Difficile. So, on one hand her death was unexpected and her cause of death short, but her health and energy had been declining quite dramatically the last year of her life. Mom had significant heart and lung disease, the treatment of which reduced her kidney function.

"I was the oldest daughter, and family dynamics being what they were, I had been actively involved in my parent's care since they moved to Colorado in 1999. My responsibilities varied from quite hands on to overseeing and coordinating care. Dad passed away June 2006. So, in summary, my caregiving role was long term with an acute illness bringing Mom's death rather suddenly.

"I remember a number of conversations with Mom the last year of her life about her being very tired, and I had told her she did not need to keep fighting to live for me. She had her doubts about how my sister and brother would handle her death. As believers it became natural to focus on heaven, resurrection bodies, being with Jesus, and being reunited with Dad. I truly know the Spirit told me that my job was to walk Mom to the gates of Heaven.

"I remember the exhaustion of being a caregiver to my Mom, Dad and Uncle; being an active baby-sitting grandmother, a wife, and mother to our adult children. So often I felt I did an inadequate job in all areas of everything. If I focused on one area the others all suffered. There was never enough time or energy to go around. One day with great guilt I confessed to my husband that I had been thinking how much easier my life would be when I no longer had to care for Mom. It sounded horrible then, and it sounds just as horrible now as I write it. So, how then did it feel like when Mom passed suddenly? That she passed too quickly? Perhaps, even when you think you are prepared, ready for your loved one to pass, you never really can be.

"There are a few very powerful memories of the last few days of Mom's life I really must tell. When Mom came home from the hospital when she had the GI bug, she came home on home hospice care; she said she did not want to go back to the hospital again. When she became acutely ill less than a week later, the hospice nurse suspected C Diff and said it might be treatable in the hospital with large doses of antibiotics. Mom indicated she wanted to go and try to treat this infection. My daughter Jennifer, who is a nurse joined Mom and I in the emergency room a few hours later. Jennifer told me soon after arriving, and more clearly than the doctors had, that Mom was in septic shock and that she would not survive and that I should stop all treatment. Mom's heart rate and blood pressure were erratic; I made the difficult decision to continue treatment, telling the doctor his job was to keep Mom alive until my brother and sister could travel to Colorado.

"While we were in the ER my eldest son Michael called and asked if Amah (his name for his grandmother) wanted anything form her apartment, and I asked him to bring some pictures of Mom and Dad, as well as her picture of Jesus. When Michael arrived with the pictures I held the pictures for her to see, and she placed her open palm on the picture of Jesus (from the book *Heaven is for Real*) and she said, 'Oh, my Jesus!' Then she looked at all of my children, their spouses, my husband and me and said, 'You all need to know I am not afraid to die.' A little while later our Pastor came, prayed with and for Mom. While he was there visiting, I looked at the 'snacks' the nursing staff had left for Mom, and lo and behold, it was crackers and grape juice. With Mom's Anglican upbringing, and her deep appreciation of her Saviors' atoning death, Communion held a special place in her heart. I asked Mom if she would like Pastor to give her communion, which we all got to witness. What a holy moment. I realized after Mom had passed away that her last Communion was her last meal as well.

"Over the next two and half days Mom's body slowly lost the battle with C Diff. We had the opportunity for some family healing, during this time, and while Mom could not speak for long, everyone got to say their goodbyes. During this time we moved Mom to an inpatient hospice centre that was incredibly supportive and helpful to all of us.

The last night of Mom's life, signs of imminent death progressed. My sister Lynda and I were with Mom, everyone else saying they were okay with not being there at the actual moment of death. Most of the time Mom was sleeping, waking only with pain or when it was necessary to clean her up. Forty-five minutes before Mom actually passed the nurses came in to reposition her and to see if she needed cleaning up. In hindsight I think they were waking her on purpose to give us some time with her awake. What a blessing that turned out to be. Mom could not speak, but she remained awake the entire time. My sister and I, one on each side of her bed were able to express our love and appreciation to her, speak of the Lord and say our goodbyes. My sister really was the only one, the perfect one I would have wanted to share those moments with. Mom was very attentive to us, and with her eyes able to let us know she heard and understood everything we were saying.

"The last few minutes Mom's attention was not on Lynda and I, her eyes were open incredibly wide, lit up, and her eyebrows were raised. She was obviously seeing something incredible! I told her I was jealous and wished I could see what she was seeing. We held Mom's hand and literally walked with her to the gate of Heaven. I firmly believe Mom was beholding the glory of God those last few minutes of her life. How wonderful was the Lord to let her see where she was going, or who she was going with, before she actually left this earth. How blessed Lynda and I were, and are, to be able to see it through Mom's eyes. It reminds me of seeing the sunlight through a crack in the door, and of the scripture, 'For now we see in a mirror dimly, but then face to face; now I know in part but then I will know fully just as I also have been fully known.' **(1Cor 13:12.)** We were witnesses of Mom's first glimpses face to face.

"*What Helped?*

My loss was, and is, huge, but I am comforted by the experience of Mom's passing. I do not question that she is in Heaven with the Lord and that one day I will be reunited with her.

"Secondly, and to me surprisingly, the actual rituals of her funeral and burial were helpful. The morning of her funeral, I was anxious, stressed out and exhausted. We had ten out of state and country house guests. The funeral was at my home church, and once again I was the primary care giver. It fell to me to be the primary organizer of all things. I was anxious that the service and the whole day honour Mom and God. The traditions, our culture, funeral service, burial service, family and friends coming together and sharing memories really did help.

"After everyone left town I emptied Mom's apartment, and while that was emotionally and physically exhausting, it was helpful that I got to do it on my own. A few weeks later, my immediate responsibilities handled, I collapsed. For about three months all I wanted to do was hibernate. Two things helped during this time. One, my husband was very understanding and did not demand or expect what I did not have to give. Secondly, I took advantage of some grief counselling through hospice. It was very helpful for me to hear that everything I was experiencing was normal.

I am in fact doing better now, ten months later. I seldom have the desire to hibernate now. Christmas was difficult, as was Mom's birthday. I tried to focus on all the good memories, and less on the loss I felt. I think I am slowly, and rather quietly dealing with feelings, and with God's help, healing is coming.

"Things that did not help? *Interesting question!* Mostly people, meaning well, telling me not to feel certain things like guilt, which, by the way the grief counsellor tells me *all* caregivers experience to some degree. The other thing that I found not only not helpful but quite negative was being told I needed medication and counselling. Once again, I am sure that person meant well, but I really needed someone to listen, not tell me I was screwed up and needed fixing!

"The most understanding people I found were ones who had experienced a significant loss themselves. This is something I am trying to remember myself as I try to comfort others who are grieving. I have found there is a bit of a sisterhood, or club of other women who have recently experienced a death, something I think I should not shy away from but embrace for my own benefit and that of others.

"One rather significant thing that I believe God is showing me is the sometimes huge gap between what I say, I believe, and my emotions. One example of this is my feelings of guilt. I have confessed and asked for forgiveness for my attitudes, and thoughts of being burdened by my caregiving role, and for some specific things I did not do for Mom during her last few weeks of life. I say I believe that when I confess and ask forgiveness it is granted and the issue is over. Sometimes I still feel guilt. The gap between my feelings and what I say I believe is troubling. Another perhaps more significant example is that I say I believe God is sovereign, that He alone numbers our days. Therefore, He knew and ordained the number of days for Mom, and allowed her to die when and how she did. If I really believe this, why do I sometimes want to blame the health care workers who did not care for her, allowing her to get dehydrated and needing to go to the hospital, where she contracted the C Diff that killed her? Once again a troubling gap . . .

"One thing I say I believe about God that has not been a struggle is when I say I believe He can take care of all my needs; this one I realize is true. I still miss Mom, but in His grace and mercy He has met all my needs. As I focus on the truth of whom and all God is, He is able to meet even more."

From Kirstin – In memory of her full term, perfectly formed son Coby.

My sons have known Kirstin and her husband Jason since Elementary School.

"January 3, 2013, the date my beautiful baby boy Coby was born still. Tuesday night, at almost forty-one weeks, I went into labour and Coby was moving around being his normal self. Wednesday morning when the midwives arrived, we couldn't find a heartbeat. Thursday afternoon, after an hour and twenty minutes of pushing, my beautiful, nearly ten-pound baby boy was born. He was so beautiful and so perfect with his mommy's hands. We held him, our families held him and we held him some more. Then we said goodbye.

"Today, words started to come to me and I knew it was time to sit and write. I created a post on Facebook. It's only the tiniest bit of an enormous and overwhelming experience, but it helps to put something into words. I hope it's okay that I share it here – it's a little long. It all happened so fast and seems so surreal that I just needed to post it somewhere, to say, this has happened and here's how I'm doing. I've read so many posts here and my heart breaks for every loss I read about and I am so sad that there is a need for a place like this to exist, but I am so thankful it does. It was nearly three weeks ago, or not even three weeks ago, I'm not sure which one is easier to say, and I'm in my living room surrounded by the flowers that should have welcomed him. Instead they are here as reminders of a goodbye that we never anticipated. Not even three weeks ago, as we prepared to say hello, we learned we were instead going to be saying goodbye to our beautiful little boy, Coby.

"Every day I wake up and life feels normal. We never brought him home, there are no memories of him in the bassinet by our bed, no memories of midnight feedings and diaper changes, no memories of family cuddles in our bed with our dog sniffing at his new playmate. It is just a home being prepared for the arrival of a baby. Just space waiting to be filled with love, laughter and warmth. Just a void that will never be filled. Even if/when we have other children, the space for Coby, our firstborn son, will always be a space. So, I wake up every day and life is the same as it was before he was born and it feels normal, familiar. Then I remember that it shouldn't, life should be so vastly different and I spend the rest of the day reconciling the life I should have with the life I'm actually living. The journey through each day is different. Every moment presenting different emotions that wash over me as though I am standing in the middle of an ocean. A wave of guilt, a wave of sadness, a wave of peace, a wave of happiness, a wave of heartbreak. Each wave a different colour, a different texture, sometimes just covering my toes, sometimes a giant tsunami, never washing over me in the same way. Sometimes they catch me off guard and sometimes I can see it coming, a particular wave, off in the distance, reaching towards me. I never run from it, maybe because I know there is nowhere to go. I just stand there and let it wash over me and through me. I breathe it in, wondering if I will drown in it, but I never do. Sometimes the wave stays for a while, sometimes it is gone as quickly as it arrives, but each one somehow leaves me changed, a little more healed, a little less broken.

"So I remember my beautiful baby boy Coby every day. I remember how carrying him in my womb has changed me, how losing him has changed me. I remember how much his little life has in every possible way changed me forever and I try to honour him by striving to be the kind of woman, the kind of Mom that would make him proud.

"I love you, Coby, my sweet angel, my beautiful little man. I love you, today and every day."

From Elsje, Coby's Grandmother who I have known for twenty-five years.

Grief has brought us a little more closely together again.

"Moments in Time."

"Tomorrow it is two months since Coby's death and birth. Today Kirstin showed me the pictures that were taken right after he was born. They were beautiful and heartbreaking all at the same time. It seemed strange at the time but I am so grateful that they were taken; it helps to make it real, to know that he was with us and that it happened. It was comforting to see his little face again; I didn't really want to put them down, it made me feel a little like he was still with us. It brought back all of the moments that we went through.

"It is a series of moments that stay in my mind that make up what happened. The moment I heard the midwives struggling to find Coby's heartbeat, the moment that Kirstin came into the living room to tell me that they were going to the hospital and the look on her face, I could see her trying to process what was happening. The moment that she phoned me from the hospital to say that the news wasn't good. The moments of making phone calls to tell Chuck (Kirstin's father), her brother Andrew and his wife Kim, and Kirstin's sister Rachel that Coby had died, and the moment that I saw Kirstin in the hospital.

"Then the moments of waiting strung together while everyone arrived at the hospital and the looks of disbelief that passed over everyone's face: 'How is this possible?' 'Everything was fine.' 'This can't be true.' Then came the moments of gathering information, what was going to happen next, why did this happen. After a long and sleepless night the moments of watching Kirstin go through the final stages of labour, walking away from the door thinking *I can't listen to my daughter push her dead baby out.* Then came the first moment etched permanently in my brain of seeing a grief stricken Jason holding his dead son in his arms as the door to their room opened for a brief moment. Then came the moments of seeing a drugged and exhausted Kirstin with her son, of all of us taking our turn to hold him and say our goodbyes and giving him the only kisses we were ever going to be able to give him. My heart was broken, how could this be, this beautiful baby boy, so perfect with his chubby cheeks, with Kirstin's hands, this beautiful long awaited baby.

"Then there are the moments of helping Kirstin and Jason plan their son's funeral and of watching Kirstin, still weak from the delivery and Jason graciously greeting the many people who came to wish them well at the visitation. Kirstin and Jason showed endless openness and inclusion and tremendous wisdom through every step from the moment they knew their dear son had died, through the delivery, to the steps of planning the funeral.

"I had to start coming to the realities of my grief as Coby's grandmother, but I also had to watch my other children move through their own processes of grief. You know as a mother that you can't protect your children from the pain of this life but it goes against every fibre of my being to have to watch my children deal with devastating loss. There are those moments of conversation in the early days as I tried to gauge how they were managing while I tried to come to grips with the reality of the tragedy that had befallen all of us. There are the moments of supporting Rachel as she tried to understand her emotions and was unsure of what to feel and feeling helpless to support her sister, and the moments of talking with Andrew and Kim as they processed through their anger and grief and the unfairness of what had happened. There are the moments of tentative phone calls, the first conversations with Kirstin and Jason, bringing dinner to their home and seeing them curled together under the quilt that I had made for Coby. I added the fabric that was meant for the wraps that were supposed to carry him to make the quilt big enough for the two of them to cover themselves with.

"Two months have passed, my grief is still fresh, I cry easily, I tire easily, my heart beaks every time again when I hear and see Kirstin and Jason travelling through their grief. I have moments where I am sad and moments when I am angry and feel robbed. Robbed of the phone calls from an exhausted Kirstin because Coby was up all night and, 'Could I come and take him for a while so she can have a nap?' Robbed of watching Kirstin and Jason grow as parents. I have seen Kirstin become a mother, she knows now what it is to give birth, to love a child that is yours and I feel robbed, as does she, of being able to have the joy of that knowledge. I feel robbed of the joy of having Grandma Time and playing with him and having the secrets about our adventures that only Coby and I would have. Of watching him become the child and eventually the man he was supposed to be. I feel robbed of the Grandma bragging rights that I was supposed to have, of all of his misadventures and adventures of his accomplishments and his struggles. Then there are the moments that I am exhausted and I think, it is what it is, I can't change it, I just need to find peace with it. Then there are those moments when life takes me away from the reality, I have a deadline to meet at work, another meeting to go to, another email to answer, and then there is that moment at the end of a hectic work day when I drive back to my empty house that I remember: *Ah yes, there it is, the hole in my heart for the one that was but is no longer.*

"I allow myself the moments that I become engrossed in my day and can smile and enjoy what I am involved in. I also allow myself the moments of anger and sadness and the flow of tears that feel like they will never stop. I know this is all part of the process and that the moments of sadness and heartache will grow farther apart; but right now and especially today, those moments are close together and the peaceful moments tend to be more elusive than present.

"I know it is a journey; I have travelled the journey of grief before; I recognize it and remember the process. I know it will grow softer and easier, that it won't seem so fresh and raw, that when we talk about Coby my heart won't ache as much. I also know that he will always have a place in our lives, he will always be missed and we will always wonder who he would have become. I also find my moments of peace in my shared moments with Kirstin and Jason, I am grateful that they have let me be a part of their journey, that they have been open and shared. I know this would have been so much more difficult if it had not been for the fact that I have been able to be so connected. It is one thing to grieve for your own loss but it is a whole other thing to watch your children grieve the loss of their own child and knowing that their reality is that much more difficult and their grief is that much deeper. When I see that they are as okay as can be expected and that they are moving through their grief, I have peace. At least I know they are going to be okay, that they won't lose themselves in the process that they will move through it and get to the other side.

"I will remember Coby always; not only as the one who was, but also as the one who we gathered together for and who showed us how much of a family we are and how we can support each other. I will remember Coby as the one who showed me that my children are strong and that they are resilient, that they are wise and capable. I will remember Coby as the one who reminded me of the importance of good and strong relation- ships, who brought a different level of connection for me with Kirstin. I will remember Coby as the one who turned Kirstin and Jason into parents. I will remember Coby as a beautiful baby who we had for a moment."

A Word about Bereavement Support Groups

I am well aware that support groups aren't for everyone. That is most evident by the fact that each year, we have served an average of ten to twelve people per group in our spring and fall programs. Tallman Funeral Homes usually serve over 300 families a year, which affirms rather soundly the above statement about groups. But for the five to eight percent of people who do reach out and attend, I believe I can say with credibility that our group does help.

One Step at a Time bereavement support programs began in 1994. There have been a couple of facilitators come and go, but a strong core of five of us have walked alongside hundreds of people in grief since we began the group. We have learned much along the way and have vowed that the moment we think we have arrived and know it all, it will be time to pass the torch.

One of the most important things we learned early was to bring together the two groups that are run each year for one night the following January. Most of these people have encountered the Christmas season for the first time without their loved one. We discovered they are eager to come back together to talk about that, reconnect and explore further what their new life is like for them.

I am always intrigued by the ease with which the two groups come together, the raw honesty that is spoken and the level of hope identified and shared. One year seventeen people showed up for our mini reunion. The chatter as people gathered was delightful. No, it wasn't necessarily buoyant but the presence of the precious camaraderie that had grown out of a time of great need for support emanated. Most people's natural self-presentation bore the promise of hope while a few, whose grief was still just months new, demonstrated that uncharted territory affect. Grief had been their bed partner for a while, but not long enough for their loved one to recess more comfortably to the place of memory that would naturally need to happen.

We shared our different Christmas experiences. A few new rituals were tried with differing levels of success and contentment. Several sounded surprised at how well things went, while others had spent a more quiet and lonely time. It was New Year's Eve that many echoed as being more challenging. "I couldn't say Happy New Year to my husband" or "This was the first New Year's Eve in forty years that my husband and I didn't celebrate together." Jackie couldn't say enough about how her kids came together and worked hard to make Christmas meaningful. The presence of her eight-month-old grandchild (the happiest baby she has ever seen) brought joy. Hannah, whose son had died after years of developmental and medical issues, surprised me the most. When she attended the spring group, every ounce of her tiny self was wracked with raw, unbearable grief. This night, several months later, she had a bright clarity and a sense of purpose in her face that could not be denied. She spoke of revisiting a routine she and Martin had all his life where he would expect her to say "Good morning" to all his stuffed animals. At Christmas, she lined up

Cookie Monster, Big Bird and the gang in Martin's room and wished them all a Merry Christmas just as she and Martin would have done. For Hannah, that helped. She also shared with me as we were saying goodbye that she has started some volunteer work with Family and Children's Services, which had brought purpose back into her life.

There were questions such as "What do I do about the 'what ifs' and the 'regrets' that still haunt me?" As much as Adeline had a wonderful Christmas in Winnipeg, she still had to come home to a dark, cold and lonely house where those questions would continue to plague her. She spoke about talking to her husband's picture. A few people suggested writing, journaling, scribing a letter to her husband. But it was priceless to hear our youngest facilitator Jo-Anne suggest to Adeline that if talking to her husband's picture is helpful, keep doing it, because not everyone is a journalist or likes to write. Thank you, Jo-Anne.

Time and the length it takes for someone to come back to themselves through reconciliation of their loved one's death was talked about at length. Many had heard that year two could be worse for them than the first year and that caused angst. I had to confess to them that was my reality. Mary spoke of it being a full four years before she knew she was going to be okay. Others who had attended our groups in the past have cited anywhere from two to seven years before they could say with confidence that life had returned to some sense of normal, control and peace. Carol expressed concern around people feeling sorry for themselves during Christmas at the expense of losing focus on the very reason for Christmas, celebrating the birth of Christ. And yes, for those with faith, the promise of the Son of God being born in a feeding stall for us is something to embrace, even in grief. But we also had to agree that if we didn't feel and acknowledge the sadness and the rougher times, we wouldn't know their opposites of joy and peace. We couldn't ignore also that we were hearing hope in that room, some expressed with a measure of confidence while others could barely whisper it. I learned earlier in the week at a funeral that the Greek definition of hope is assurance. That is a word full of promise and confidence. At almost exactly the same moment, facilitator John echoed what was in my mind to ask him, to offer a prayer. *Perfect!*

Bring seventeen people together in various seasons of grief and allow them to share what's in their hearts in a safe environment and we can't help be reminded that hope (assurance) is always on the map. Again, whether it is the love of practically strangers, family, friends, or God, *love wins!*

Chapter 11

Tributes to Rick Bear

With an element of uncertainty, I have included this chapter, which is all tributes paid to my husband Rick. It may, however, appear to some readers as if I am 'one of those people' who, in grief, puts their loved one on an indestructible pedestal. There are two answers to that possible reaction: the first being *no*. My grief has included acknowledging our less than perfect relationship, but we remained committed to work at it together for a lifetime.

The second reason is more from a desire to emphasize the value of good teachers, and Rick was an amazing one, and pay homage to the honourable profession of education.

At a time when teachers and government are at logger heads in our province (and I have no idea who has the better argument), the privilege of educating young minds is still that. And it would appear by the student comments included here that Mr. McBay conveyed well to his students that he indeed saw teaching and learning together with young people as a privilege. *Was he perfect?* Hardly. There were times when he had a bit of an edge but overall, he loved being with his students, and he loved coming home to tell me about those 'light bulb' moments he loved to witness.

As in any profession, there are stellar employees and then the not so stellar. Probably anyone growing up through an education system can attest to some pretty poor teachers or professors. But I am convinced we could each speak to that one or couple of teachers who made a difference or turned the light bulb on for us. Mine was Mr. McLaughlin for Grade

13 Creative Writing. The value of words my father taught me came to life in Mr. McLaughlin's class.

Included here then are my words given at Rick's funeral where my brother stood at my side. Following are just a few of hundreds of comments written by students in a memory book created by the staff at Great Lakes Christian High School.

December 16, 2010 – My funeral tribute to my husband of thirty-five and a half years in the presence of 700 people, after eighty plus Great Lakes Chorus members past and present sang 'The Greatest Commands':

"I said to Noel at the hospital moments after Rick died, 'Imagine what he is seeing right now,' and I entitled this tribute that, but imagine what he is hearing right now!

"I thank you for being here, and there's been tons of phone calls and emails, with so many emails I haven't been able to respond to. I hope to do so, but it might take a while.

"I don't know how many times over the past few days that Brian, Shanna, Terral, Laura and I have been reminded of the impact Rick seems to have had on literally hundreds of people. I also don't know how many times I have said he would be humbled and *freaked out* by all this attention. Because I believe one of God's greatest felt presence is through his people, we are obviously deeply loved and I too am overwhelmed.

"My tribute to my husband Rick Bear may be a bit self-serving and I won't apologize for that, but I hope you will understand that it is a part of our healing as a family. When we were planning this wonderful gift of remembrance and praise for Rick and to God, I kept expressing concern that we not make it too long. Well, we've totally failed on that. But my daughter-in-law Laura wisely observed that after all the wonderful expressions of grief and loss we have been reading since late Saturday night, it is finally our turn. Please know that we also lift up all that has been offered to a God we know loves us and is somehow hurting with us.

"After those unbelievable moments when a most wonderful nurse who accompanied Rick from Grimsby to Hamilton General Hospital broke protocol and came to tell me that he had died, it was so very good to have my dear friend Carole with me. When Noel arrived and we were trying to work through that initial shock, I was quite able to say, 'Imagine what he is seeing right now in heaven.'

"Another most dear friend Laurena could not wait to come home on Sunday morning to tell us about the wonderful time of worship here at this church that our church family had. They put aside the sermon and plans they had for that Sunday morning, gave opportunity for people to sing and share stories about Rick. *How awesome is that!* Laurena also needed to tell us about an experience her mother had at a presentation of Messiah, the same night Rick died. Mother Anna and sister Caroline during the Hallelujah chorus truly felt that someone was being lifted up to God, and when they heard about Rick's death happening around the same time that wonderful chorus was being sung, Anna wanted to know the moment Rick died and was it him being lifted up to God. The choir who has sung the Hallelujah chorus many times put their books down and sang it like they never had before. Mum Anna also knows about the loss of a husband and I may need to lean on her at some point.

"What seems really important to say today is to acknowledge my, our grief, at this huge loss, tell you a bit about my love for Rick and to let you know just how deeply he loved God. As I asked students and teachers in Chapel at Great Lakes this week, I ask you *not* to be afraid of me. In bereavement work, I have heard many times, more than I would like how people are afraid to support someone like me. What will you say, what can you do? Please, don't let that stop you from giving hugs, talking about Rick, letting me cry when needed, offering to stop by and include me, when I am ready, in social functions and please be willing to do the same for my family.

"The fact that the Hamilton Male Police Chorus , *not* choir, which Rick directed for seventeen years were willing to come and sing two years after that retirement is icing on the cake. When Rick was being interviewed for the position and when he was hired, one of the first things he asked was, 'When do I get my gun?' Of course he didn't get the gun, but he had a lot of fun with you guys and he had the unique ability to command you when needed. Just think about that for a second.

"Rick Bear, thirty-eight years of memories, love, struggle, joy, contentment with our home and property, service to God, shaping students to become successful and Christ seeking young human beings; how can we not be proud of that? But he too, like the rest of us had his imperfections and quirks. Just get Brian and Terral started on some of those and it could become quite entertaining. I love him deeply. Sometimes I feel like I didn't love him enough and yet we both knew solace, peace, safety, joy and sorrow in the love that we shared.

"What the heck am I going to do with all the stuff he collected over the years, which at times cause us to curse him; actually Terral and I already have. Finally, I wish to speak to his love and commitment to his God and church. As our minister Noel blogged very early Sunday morning, Rick wasn't content to do what we had always done. He was always trying things. 'If you're going to do it, do it big and huge and fantastic, and do it right!' I know from experience that his zeal for God, the church and meaningful worship which meant change, was not well received by some. My prayer today is that I can impart on those that are uncertain about his motives, that his love for Jesus was very real, very passionate and it sometimes blew me out of the water. He was learned in the Bible. His university degrees were in Music and Religious Studies. His work over the years in the church, most recently as an elder taught him a sense of grace, which helped him become more sensitive and compassionate towards those struggling with change. But you also have to know that sometimes it drove him crazy not to be able to do things he just knew would be wonderful for the church.

"Young people often get it much sooner than we more advancing folks and they have much to teach us. For the students at Great Lakes where Rick taught, I am so very proud of the wisdom of the staff to meet together first to get their heads around the loss, and then provide opportunity for the student body to voice their grief. Astoundingly, a two-hour assembly on Monday before classes began was full of those precious young people who are all here today, offering tribute to their teacher, chorus director, play director, computer guy, Mr. Fix It and friend. Their comments they offered, their desire to sing today for Mr. McBay demonstrate to me at least their knowledge that he loved them, he wanted them to know the love of God and that they needed to thank Him for his love, trust and grace.

"Maybe in the darker hours of January and February I may find myself asking the question, 'Why now?' *I'm not sure.* Right now I know that I am somewhat numb, but I also know how much I miss Rick and I also know it's not just about my loss. My sons Brian and Terral, Shanna and Laura and our precious grandbabies are missing and will continue to miss Papa. I realize by the presence of all of you here today that Rick impacted your life in some way and I am humbled. But the work that I do reminds me on a daily basis that maybe it should be instead, 'Why not?' *We will all die.* Yes it truly is a part of life. While we have celebrated Rick here today, I can think of other things I would rather celebrate. The very last words Rick uttered on Saturday to the radiologist after he and I had said 'I love you' at least a couple of times throughout the day were, 'We place ourselves in your hands.' Rick has been taken from us, much sooner than any of us would have liked and there will be days when this is extremely painful and it already has been. But for now, I do not ask 'Why?' or 'Why now?' but instead ask: 'Lord, be with me and my family.'

"My sister found this prayer with which I would like to end these comments and it is by that famous author – Unknown.

" *'We trust that beyond absence there is presence*
That beyond the pain there can be healing
That beyond the brokenness there can be wholeness
That beyond the anger there may be peace
That beyond the hurting there may be forgiveness
That beyond the silence there may be the word
That beyond the word there may be understanding
That through understanding there is love.'"

Comments of Love and Appreciation from Students at Great Lakes Christian High School.

These have been scribed as they were written in a memory book.

From Mack, Grade 11:

"Mr. McBay, you were such an inspiring person in my life. You taught me in many classes and I learned more about myself sometimes than the subject. You looked at me once and simply said, 'Mack, life is not a joke, you have to take it seriously.' I believe you lived life in that manner. You got all you could from every day, bringing joy to our hearts. The last thing you said to me was that you were so proud of me. That means so much to hear from such a great man. I wish I had time to tell you how much I appreciate and cherish your kindness and love. You were more than a teacher, sir, you were a strong Christian, a mentor and someone I looked up to. You always said what needed to be heard and I give you tremendous respect for that."

From Christella, Grade 10:

"Dear, Mr. McBay, I know you are not here anymore, and you won't be able to read this physically, but I know you'll know how much I miss you. Somehow, you know that I'm writing this, right? GL really depends on you a lot, you are so important to this school. I haven't had a chance to take your music class yet; how is that fair? It's so sad to think that I have never written you a letter before. This is my first time writing to you, but it is too late. You're not going to read it and give me feedback. Thank you so much for always saying good things to me and making me feel like I'm worth something, like I'm important. You really show that you love us and that touches me. It's terrible that you have to leave us so soon, but it's wonderful to think of where you're going. Thank you for giving me the ability to sing, to be humble like you are. You taught me so much more than History, Civics and Computer. You showed us how to live like Christ, you were a great example. You are loved and missed by so many people. I'm just one of them."

From Allen, Grade 11:

"Dear, Mr. McBay. There are really no words for me right now to say. There are so many things going on in my mind but I just don't know what words to use to express my feelings. You were more than just a great teacher to me, probably like for most people in GL. You have touched so many lives and I thank God so much that I was one of them. You taught me so much and not just the academic stuff in class. You taught me life lessons that I could not learn from anyone else. I used to be such a shy person and I would just usually keep to myself. Then I joined Chorus and you saw the potential in me and you never gave up until I showed it. You didn't teach me how to sing; you taught me how awesome God is and how to praise Him through singing. You have helped me in my life in so many ways, especially spiritually. And I thank you so much for that. The last few days have been rough. Sandy and I would always see you and visit you during our spare in the computer lab during fourth period and it was awesome to just chill with you. We heard the news and we were obviously sad but then when we go up to the lab on Monday for our spare and saw an empty chair, we just completely lost it. We really miss you. You always said that I did an amazing job whatever I did and told me to do better every time. I want to say thank you again."

From Chinwe, Grade 9:

"Mr. McBay. You were a selfless, optimistic, intelligent and fun man to be around in the class and in the halls. I know I am only in Grade 9, but you have had an amazing influence on me, the students and the teachers as well. You taught many lessons like how to be patient. I really enjoyed the way you loved to sing and how you always sang with a smile on your face. I will never forget your wit and sense of humour and how you could always turn a boring lesson into a fun experience."

From Sandy, Grade 11, whom I allowed to call me Sandy for obvious reasons:

"Hey, Sandy, I just wanted to express the gratitude I have for Rick's invest-ment in me. Without the effort put forth by him and his fellow teachers I would not be the man I am, I would not have the faith in my salvation that I do have. He was a beacon of joy in my life. I can remember meeting him before I started high school for the first time on the sidelines of one of GL's soccer games. He asked me if I could sing to which I replied *No*, which he took with a silence and a look that said, *We'll see about that*. It's true, somehow he taught me to sing pretty average. From his patience in Chorus to his dedication to the students, his love for music and his passion for teaching, Rick McBay truly was a beacon of God's love and a wonder-ful example of Christ's call for self-sacrifice."

A final reason to include this chapter of tributes is to honour the words of my son Brian, written for his father at his funeral. Terral's homage to his father that day was to end the service with a 'go big or go home' leading of 'O Holy Night'.

From my son Brian, December 16, 2010 – Rick's Funeral

"Well, I'm not a huge fan of Facebook but in the last few days, I have come to appreciate it (and the visitation times yesterday) for this reason: people have been freely sharing memories of Dad . . . memories that I didn't know about. In the last few days, I have learned about Dad's impact as a teacher, elder, mentor, Scout leader, brother, uncle, friend, community member and choral conductor. I always had inklings of his profound impact on others through these various roles, but clearly did not know the full extent, the vast scope of his influence. It's a shame we don't share great memories of each other on a regular basis . . . that it often takes a death before people engage this way. But I'm so happy to know how others saw dad. And I'm fiercely proud of the man he was and the impact he had on so many. Today I want to share memories of Dad that will perhaps expand your impression of who he was. I want to share about Dad as a father.

"There are many memories to choose from.

One of my earliest memories is of Dad taking me on long bike rides in the evenings. I was probably between the age of two and four because I was still sitting on the bike seat directly behind him. He did all the work; all I had to do was hold on and enjoy the ride. I remember the first half of those rides usually included looking around at the scenery as it floated by; talking and laughing with Dad, and being exhilarated by how fast we were going. The ride home was usually a different story. By that time, I was getting tired, and it was getting colder. In response, I would first put my hands and then my whole head under Dad's shirt. I would cuddle up as close as possible to catch his warmth, and I would rest. The feelings that I retain from those rides home are ones of complete joy and utter contentment at being this close to my Dad; feeling so special and loved; feeling safe and entirely without concern, because I was with my Dad and he had everything under control.

"Dad was strong. Terral and I were commenting on the size and strength of his hands as we were holding them after he died. Dad had meat glove hands and sausage fingers. He was unbelievably strong. The first time I noticed this was when I was in Beaver's as a boy. We were building a bird house, and Dad was actually letting me do some of the hammering. I bent one of the nails, and then watched as he hooked his thumb underneath the nail, and casually bent it back straight. I knew then that he was the strongest man in the world. When we got older, Dad would challenge Terral and I to finger wrestles. Dad would hold out his hands, one of us would link our fingers between his, and then we would finger wrestle until someone called uncle. Dad always won. Over the years as I got older (and presumably stronger) I would challenge him to a rematch, thinking, *Surely I'm stronger than he is now . . . I'm in my prime, and he's getting old.* To this date, I have never won one of those finger wrestles, and clearly I never will.

"I have clear memories of Dad teaching me how to catch and hit a ball. This took some time to master, but he was always patient, and always encouraging.

"Later, he would coach both Terral and I in baseball, and I remember that he was always a fierce advocate for us as players and for our teams. Part of being an advocate meant that occasionally he would inform the umpires that they had made a bad call. Dad was always very creative in the ways he would phrase these comments. He never swore, and yet the timing and phrasing were always enough to make those of us on the bench blush and turn to each other and say, 'Is he allowed to say that?'

"This next memory stays with me because it made me see Dad in an entirely different way. You all will remember him as a leader. Dad was always in charge, telling people what to do, delegating tasks, answering questions. Dad was an authority figure. He wore that role well. So, a few summers ago at a family reunion with his brother and sisters and cousins in Bracebridge, I was surprised to see Dad as a little brother. Dad is the youngest sibling in his family. I remember watching him around his family, weaving in and out around his older siblings, almost giddy in his interactions with them. He looked up to them. His actions demonstrated a desire to serve and even impress them, and he looked incredibly happy to be with them, as the baby brother. I had never seen Dad like that before. It shook me a bit, and at the time, I remember even feeling a bit embarrassed for him, because this seemed so out of character. But it was just a different part of his character, shaped from a young age. And I look back on that now fondly.

"Since having children, I'm learning the many levels and implications of what it means to be a father. I remember Dad telling me on many occasions, 'You never stop being a Dad; you never stop worrying; you never stop waiting up until you know your children are safe at home; you never stop being proud of your kids, you never stop wanting to hold them, and comfort them, and keep them safe.' Last summer, Shanna and I were at Mom and Dad's for a visit with our kids, Carter and Haley. At one point during this visit, Carter, Dad and I were all sitting on the swing in the back yard. Carter was leaning back against the cushions and he put his feet up on my lap. Dad saw this, and said to me, 'Do you want to put your feet up on my lap, too?' If he had asked me this a few years ago, before I had kids, I would have looked at him funny and said, 'No thanks, I'm alright.' But on this occasion, I looked at him, and began remembering all those things he told me about what it means to be a father. Just because I am now a father, doesn't mean that he has stopped being mine. 'Do you want to put your feet up on my lap, too' wasn't just an idle request to create a pretty picture on the swing. He wanted to have that physical connection with his son, and let me know that he was there for me, and loving me and keeping me safe. And he wanted me to relax and let down my guard and be his little boy again. And so I did. I put my feet on his lap, and leaned back into the cushions, while my son did the same with me. And it *was* a pretty picture, it was a special moment, and we all felt great, and whole, and content.

"These next few memories are from Saturday. So, get out your Kleenexes if you haven't already, and, Pastor Mike, if you aren't already reading, get ready, because this might be the end of the line for me.

"I will never forget Mom calling me on Saturday night, telling me that Dad had a seizure and crashed. That she needed her sons there with her because she was scared.

"I will never forget arriving at the hospital with Terral, only to have Mom tell us that she had called us too late, and Dad had already gone.

"I will never forget wanting to burst into the next room where I thought he was, only to realize that it was actually a washroom, and that Dad was down the hall.

"I will never forget the way Dad looked as he lay there in the trauma room, and how he reminded me so strongly of *his* Mom when she died.

"I will never forget holding his hands, and seeing his hospital bracelet, and finally figuring out how old he was by calculating back from his birthdate.

"I will never forget my brother hugging Dad and kissing his forehead, while whispering words of love to his father.

"I will never forget Ralph Tallman coming in to see Dad before taking him back to Vineland. Terral said, 'It's not every day you see a funeral director cry.'

"I will never forget Noel Walker praying with Mom, Terral and I, trying to speak words of comfort, while at the same time struggling with his own profound grief.

"I know that Dad did not want to leave yet. He should have had many more years to spend with his wife and soul mate, with his friends and students and church, and with his children. He should have had many more years with his grandchildren. Dad was a great Papa to Carter, Haley, Leah and Seth. But, as far as Papa-hood goes, I think Dad was just getting into his prime. And he was enjoying the role even more as the grandchildren got older, and could toddle around after him, help him do chores, and bask in the wealth of his Wikipedia-like knowledge.

"I have been taking strength from my faith and the faith of my family, friends and church communities. Dad, like all of us here was a forgiven man. And Dad, like many of us here was a believer. In his life, Dad sinned, but because of Jesus, God did not see him and does not see us as sinners.

"Rather, when God looks at Dad and when he looks at us, he sees Jesus and he is very pleased with what he sees. Some people have commented that the heavenly choir has just gained another tenor. I smile when I think of Dad singing in heaven, next to those he knew and loved, and next to our dear friend Jeremy King who passed away just over a month ago. I also smile when I think of Dad approaching God after a choir practice and saying, 'Hey, if you ever need me to step in as conductor, I do have some experience . . . just sayin'.'

"Terral. We are brothers and so are united in a similar grief. I am here for you, and know that you are here for me. Dad loved you so intensely and I see a lot of Dad in you. You have his work ethic, his skill for taking things apart and putting them back together, his skill for fixing and building and making things with your hands. You have Dad's musical abilities. You have taken Dad's example of faith, and put that into practice in your own life in a very strong and effective way. I look up to you a lot. I admire your strength and who you are as a husband and a father. I love you.

"Shanna and Laura. You have been selfless servants to your husbands, children and mother-in-law. We are so grateful to you. We know this is a hard time for you also because in many ways, he was your Dad as well. And he loved you. His girls. Finally, after so many years with just us boys.

"Mum. I don't know how you've been as awesome as you've been over the last few days. You have been there for your sons and our wives and children in our grief. You have been strong for others and gracious, and you have been helping others walk through these days when they haven't had the tools to do so alone. Our hearts are broken for you, Mom. You and Dad were a great team. It was so evident that you enjoyed being together and sharing everything together. Terral and I take great comfort knowing you have such a strong support network here. Your church and friends, your school and students all have a profound love for you and will be here for you whenever you need it. Terral and I respect and honour your need to be alone with your grief for the next few days. But you also need to know that Terral and I are going to begin investing in crude oil and asphalt. We figure we'll see some return on our investment, based on how often we plan to be driving back and forth from Waterloo, burning gas and wearing down roads. We love you so much, Mom.

"Dad. I wish this hadn't happened. I miss you and have been wishing you were here over the last few days for so many reasons. I'm sure you've been surprised by the outpouring of love and support from so many people in response to your passing. And I'm sure you would have, for many reasons, been pleased with the service today. We don't know how we will go on without you. But we rejoice, knowing you are at home and at peace with your heavenly Father."

From our neighbour Danny, who met Rick and I at a difficult time in his life and now with Susan I can call a friend, humble keeper of justice and all round interesting guy:

Rick

"A leader, a follower, a friend, a neighbour . . .
a realist, a dreamer, a person, a memory . . .
too early for some, too late for others . . .
we grieve all as one.
Let's build a community of leaders, good followers, shepherds, flocks . . .

safe, helpful, sincere, grateful.
What do you do when the neighborhood leader is gone?
Look to the past, look forward, look within . . .
look deeply.
Find what he has taught you,
and make it part of yourself,
so Rick's purpose in life lives on, with Sandy,
with his children, grandchildren,
neighbourhood, church, community and country.
He stood for what was right.
And he stood firm and stood like all men should.
Now he rests in peace . . .
We know that is a better place and less worrisome than before,
because Rick went there for us, to learn,
to live and to carry on the wonder he created in the simple notion of
'a person'.
We miss you, Rick, and forever will.
And yet you will forever live within all of us always,
and in as many ways as we are fortunate to have shared and learned
with you."
– Danny Katz

Chapter 12

Year Two

Sheerly upon observation, probably most people would see me as relatively calm, assured, friendly, caring, social and perhaps even a bit outgoing. Traits such as listening, advocacy, creativity, persistence, loyalty and compassion could also be identified within me. The sum of all those parts adds up to a woman who is moving forward after her husband has died. And on the outside, all of those characteristics would be correct. Regular self-assessment, causes me to see that person others observe when I am fulfilling my responsibilities at my high school office, in the bereavement programs, at church, within my palliative teaching and in the community. But when I am at home by myself, the less assured more unsettled me takes charge. My grief is still real; it continues to surprise me and sometimes has a will of its own.

The second year without Rick had indeed been very perplexing. At twenty-two months, going to bed and waking up without Rick was still foreign. The more clinical passage of him disappearing into a place of memory from a place of presence, while necessary in moving forward, was extremely difficult. Its necessity for a healthier grief response angered me. We pledged until death do us part, yet death came too early without any warning. "But I wasn't ready to let him go," I recall saying often in our bereavement groups, that our hearts take much longer to catch up to the reality our brains have already processed. I believed that when I was saying it but it also felt a little too much like rhetoric. Rick died, he is not coming back and there is so much concrete evidence of that. Yet, it still feels so very foreign.

A few people I trust whose spouses have died are well beyond year two and each have assured me they are at a place in their new lives now where the hole is less enveloping, the comfort in their own skin is real. In completing an online survey one day, I was able to somewhat proudly answer that *yes, I am the sole owner of my home; yes I am responsible for researching a product before purchasing it,* and *yes, I will be the only one acting on those purchases.* The pride is felt from the perspective of a level of confidence that says, "I can do this." And there have been several times when I have shared that with Rick from a "Look at the character being built in me now".

From a spousal death perspective, probably the most consistent element of grief we have heard from those left behind is that of loneliness. It is the single most reason men more than women remarry, often within the first year after their wife has died. They just can't bear being alone. While I am not out to find another husband, I am painfully aware of what that loneliness feels like. The paradox is the more I am alone, and the easier it gets, the more difficult it becomes to put myself out there in any kind of social way. I have never been afraid of being alone; Rick travelled a fair bit with the choirs he directed. But this alone is very different, very permanent. When there is no flashing light on my phone at the end of many days to indicate someone has called and there are no email messages, the stark reminder is quite strong.

Rick's picture close to me in my living room cocoon area speaks of someone getting farther and farther away and sometimes I cannot compute that we were married for over thirty-five years. Apparently, this is me letting go of Rick from that place of presence. Bloody hard to do during those pseudo-alone times and it demands my continuing to move forward in a healthy, more positive way. I reflect on that second year, which was all about the end of magical thinking and the harsher reality settling in. My resilience is still there but it has tarnished a bit.

Finding balance is a goal bearing greater importance of late. Although the voice is faint and abstract, I can still hear Rick telling me to muster up some of that character building and come up with a plan. I too hear me telling myself to suck it up, get myself out there and involved, stretch beyond the familiar. I envisioned a day when I would wake up and be at peace with Rick's forever absence, I would have found new ways of inserting myself back into society, that wherever I was living at that time would be a real joy, and a sense of meaningful accomplishment would be mine.

When I succumb to self-pity, I am reminded by an outside source, or cause myself to recall that there is always someone bearing much more than I. Those in our bereavement groups are fresher in their grief; therefore I have something to offer – the wisdom of a nonjudgmental listening ear. Getting to a place where I can help others (outside of the bereavement group) is not as far away as it once felt. What I do on a daily basis in my work at the high school, teaching palliative volunteers, walking alongside others in grief, and finding or creating new traditions with my two young families and supporting my friends are all means of helping others and not to be taken lightly. But a growing dream within me is akin to checking off some of that 'bucket list', discovering there is still much more to do with my life, and contributing to society in a meaningful way.

During the spring of that second year, ten of our friends and I enjoyed another of many houseboat weekends on the Trent Canal system of north-eastern Ontario. This trip was a first for all of us in that we had always done so in the fall, and it was also our first excursion without Rick: master of the maps and ropes. Our last excursion had been two months before he died in 2010. My hesitancy was significant but it was comforting to know that we all wondered what this was going to be like without the Rick Bear.

The weekend was wonderful. A new couple joined us and enjoying the experience through Bruce and Linda's eyes was a treat. A couple of times, I found my way to a quieter place for a few moments to lament Rick's absence but otherwise I truly had fun. Laughter is guaranteed on such a trip.

We made a point on the Sunday morning of finding a glorious spot to anchor and enjoy a time or worship on the top deck of this luxury vessel. Again, Rick had historically been the one to loosely coordinate this precious time and assure we had the sacrament of communion. But as with other aspects of this holiday, others stepped up and made things happen in his absence. The beauty of our surroundings on this unusually warmer May long weekend was conducive to a great time of praising God, mostly in song. Someone suggested 'Eternal Father, Strong to Save'. I voiced my internal hesitancy without much explanation but we decided to go ahead. By the third verse I was noticing a couple of my friends in quiet tears. I stopped everything and asked, "Okay, what's going on, what are the tears?"

Jane blurted, "This was one of Rick's songs, and it was sung at his funeral." The next forty minutes or so were precious. Several acknowledged Rick's absence and how much they continued to miss him. This allowed for other things on people's hearts to be named and one of those sacred times only dear friends are courageous enough to embrace was welcomed. I concluded this time before a much anticipated yummy lunch by reading the riot act on our future together as friends. We are at a place in life where deaths are going to become more frequent, so I asked folks to each be mindful of their timing and to space things out nicely. I want to be able to give back at least some of the support they have shown me but will be able to spread myself only so thin. (To accentuate this concern, I have at the time of this writing attended over a brief month the funerals of two men who like Rick died most suddenly at the ages of sixty-three and sixty-eight.)

Early in my work of supporting others in grief, fellow facilitators and I implemented what has become an invaluable tool I learned about in one of the many conferences I attended. We entitled it a 'Timeline of Significant Life Events', which seems rather uncreative but its value is more in its outcome than name. Originally it was presented as a timeline of life's losses (death, divorce, job loss, to name a few), broken down into the decades of one's life from their earliest memory to present. Its purpose is to help us revisit and understand a little more those different losses, to reflect how or if we worked through them, and whether we learned some healthier coping strategies along the way.

Over the first few years most participants embraced this exercise and personally discovered its value. To our surprise, one woman brought her timeline homework and almost could not wait to present hers because she had made some important changes. As she began the exercise at home, she couldn't bear the number of losses she had encountered in her life and needed to feel a greater balance from her discovery. So she decided to document also the wonderful, joyful moments of life through each decade as well. *Brilliant!*

For all of us and especially those who discover that the losses have been more than plentiful, including the celebrations, reminds us that life is about both. And, in a world that can often camp a little too long on the negative, it is good for us all to be reminded of the positive. I wish I could remember this woman's name to give her due honour.

My timeline would be considered by some to be rather heavy on the losses side. My grandmothers died before I was born, a relationship I never enjoyed. Death became a little too familiar by the time I was ten years old and the fact that I was not included in any of the 'rituals' for my grandfathers, two uncles and Godfather taught me that death was not for children and not to be discussed. When my dearest friend Lee died at the age of twenty after ten years of some pretty nasty ups and downs with cancer; this was my first experience with a funeral. I vowed then that when I had children of my own there would be none of the mystery, fear and vow of silence around this final passage of life that seemed to be so very important.

Rick's death has been a teacher unlike all of the others combined. Much more recently, my use of the word 'disbelief' and phrase "It's just plain weird" is beginning to dissipate a bit, which is a healthy sign. However, the illusion that letting go of my grief was equated to letting go of Rick continued to plague me. Sadness, my companion, was beginning to seek out other unsuspecting souls and there were times when I was not sure I wanted to say goodbye to this, which had been so familiar for almost two years. *How pitiful is that?* But I refused to shut the door on the increasing moments of calm, accomplishment, joy and contentment. The joys and celebrations on my timeline felt far more plentiful and continued to remind me how precious life had been.

While the reality that my support system has declined in quantity in order for those who love me to carry on with their lives, the quality continues to embrace me. My dear cousin Diana, who I always saw as being much older and therefore more tolerant of me than anything as her junior, continues with her friend Gayle to mark special occasions by sending me the most delightful Jackie Lawson e-cards. Halloween had passed and I received a delightfully animated wooded scene with little ghosts flitting across the pond. Each time, I reply similarly with how much that little gesture brings me joy with the hope that they will continue indefinitely.

During the infamous Hurricane Sandy, the leaves had fallen during that late October, so our new houseboat cohorts Bruce and Linda came by one morning to help me get started on my acre plus of leaf raking. A job that was completed by two small groups of teens from Great Lakes Christian High School, who came by because they care about Mrs. McBay.

On Halloween, my friend Laurena included me in what has become a tradition in recent years. She provides dinner for her mother Anna and Ralph's mother Sadie while trick or treaters come calling. Both Ralph and Laurena have a most special knack of opening their home to many, and their consistency of support and love for me is quite lovely.

And while my son Brian is at a far more advanced place of reconciliation regarding his Dad's death, he continues to offer occasional and timely pearls of wisdom to his mother. While driving in the car together I commented that I was "getting better" in the context of accomplishing things I didn't have the energy or wherewithal to do in the first year.

"There is nothing to get better from, Mum," Brian responded. Such a simple statement and yet I was stunned. This is not a disease from which people get better, and while I have offered similar wisdom to many, I needed to be reminded for myself.

Terral would express his grief through the wisdom of his children and with action: emailing, calling or Skyping on a regular basis and finding ways to help his Mom here at home in his also limited time as husband and father of young children. The balance of life at home and helping their Momma is a challenge for both sons. I know they feel deeply for me but I also know their commitment to that needed balance. And, as I review these words on my two little families, I am struck again by the fact that sometimes I forget that at the still tender ages of thirty-two and twenty-eight, their Dad died. How selfish of me.

November 3, 2012. The 'Single Roses' group of women whose husbands have died got together for another potluck dinner, our fifth or sixth gathering that year. The camaraderie was evolving and solidifying with attention and intention. We were all at very different places in our new lives without our husbands. Sometimes there was the temptation by some to 'awfulize' their present circumstance more than the rest, but bless Connie for bringing us all back to the middle common ground. It was not just the wine that loosened our tongues and our hearts, we *knew* collectively what the rest of our support systems didn't understand, and this became one of a very few places to openly discuss that. Laughter was a main ingredient but we also understood our laments would be heard and embraced. *Precious.*

That same November 3, was one of those days when the light and hope within me was much more vibrant and palpable. The aftermath of hurricane Sandy had mellowed at least for us north of the border; the day was bright with sun and tangible purpose. Housecleaning has become a bit of a misnomer so when the energy to get at it begins to simmer, I need to act on it quickly before the desire escapes. I am not sure why the level of satisfaction is so great for some of us when we finally get down to it but my sense of accomplishment and pride after my flurry of activity was great. Rick and I would often go on a cleaning blitz together after a busier time for both of us. He would wash by hand the kitchen and bathroom floors to spare my back. Clean floors have a different feel to them making all things right with the world. So when I am gifted with the still rather infrequent surge of energy to clean, I am blessed with a simple but powerful sense of satisfaction. Although, I would have preferred Rick there with me.

Remembrance Day has always been important to both Rick and I. For one whose father, and two uncles served in WW II, the emotion of this day is not lost on me. Both my father and his brother were shot down over Germany, my father twice, and his fate was to spend a year in a POW camp in Barth. My other uncle served in Italy and to this day he actually recalls those days as the best of his life. Rick's passion around Remembrance Day was not familial, yet his allegiance to giving honour to veterans was fierce. Rick taught Grade 10 History and his goal was to bring to life what our ancestors experienced. Both he and I worked hard to assure that our Great Lakes students took time to pause each November 11 with an all-school assembly. Rick had an uncanny ability to empower his students to learn about and 'get' the importance of this world changing event almost seventy years past.

Thus they were eager to be creative and do the best they could to bring to life and give meaning to the thousands of lives sacrificed for our freedom. To complement the students' efforts, Rick would wear my father's RAF uniform. Sadly that year, with November 11 falling on a Sunday, there was no school assembly. While we observed two minutes of silence at

11:00 am at church, the stories, music, photos, and Flanders Fields were conspicuous by their absence.

At the best of times, November can be a bitter sweet month. The promise of Christmas with its qualities of renewal, mystery, magic and salvation through the humblest of births of a tiny child named Jesus reminds us again of hope. Yet the shorter colder days and even colder longer nights can feel ominous and overbearing when navigating depression or grief or both. On the heels of a more promising lighter time felt during that second year, I found myself suspended between giddy joy and the sadness that increased loneliness breeds.

As the third year approached, I thought that being solo would start to become easier to deal with, and not a more daunting prospect. Having said that I function just fine, yet statistics remind me I may live another twenty-five to thirty years and, if I feel this alone now, what might I be like then?

Yes, how I continue to navigate forward is my choice barring the unknown. Historically, I have chosen life, which has always blessed me, even at the darkest times, and I will continue to choose life. And yes, it would appear I have much left to give others and the gift is almost always in the giving. However, there are still daily times of yearning that Rick was here to continue life with me.

To help myself out of the oppressive loneliness, I made a couple of important decisions. Physical action, movement, is often the first on my list to bite the dust when loneliness starts to win. And with the responsibilities of summer tucked away for the winter it is really easy to become sedentary for too many months. Yoga had been on my mind for a while but the challenge of working a class into my timetable was becoming too easy an out. Finally, I bought a Yoga for Beginners DVD and discovered over the first six days that it had much to offer physically and emotionally. My living room cocoon area expanded to welcome a lovely blue yoga mat, and my cat Jake felt the need to join me in this new venture.

The renewed feeling of purpose was a nice surprise and great motivator. A guided meditation at the end of the Hatha routine took me completely by surprise. Instead of the suggested riverside in India to aid in visualization, my mind was taken to Adam Lake where my sister lives and where we McBays enjoyed time each summer over a thirty-five-year period. The beauty of this pristine little lake is committed to memory and I am able to go there easily during these meditations. Drifting around the circumference of the lake, taking in all the little bays, points, loons, heron, cottages and docks creates peace within. One particular yoga meditation was unsettlingly beautiful and most welcome. As I approached our dock around the last bend I looked up to see Rick sitting there waiting for me. It was so wonderful to see him. Crying and smiling at the same time is interesting.

My other course of action was to invite myself to be with others. If the mountain won't come to Mohammed . . .

Without giving it too much thought, I called Terral and Laura and invited myself up for the afternoon to spoil on Leah and Seth a bit. There was no hesitation at the other end of the phone so I set out after church. Grandchildren's unbridled joy to see you is almost an elixir. We had a delightful time together, some of which was spent on a walk through a most beautiful wooded area just outside of Elmira. Here was a place for Tucker the dog to run, a wonderful setting for this year's Christmas photo of this lovely little McBay family and it was all experienced through the eyes of Leah and Seth. Seth's pure joy at most discoveries is salve for the soul. The best!

But I still stumble often when it comes to stepping outside the safety of my home and my little cocoon of solace. Sometimes I find myself apologizing to friends when they learn from others about how I am 'faring', or not. Again, much of this grief is a solo act and while I relish when someone sincerely talks about Rick or genuinely asks how they can help, it is still difficult to believe that many would be interested any more. After all, it *was* two years. Many days, just a drop in the bucket.

December 7, 8 and 9, 2012

While dates are incredibly important to many in grief – me included – I found myself at the end of year two, focusing on the 'anniversary' days. Friday, December 7 was the first formal performance of the Great Lakes annual production – 'You're a Good Man Charlie Brown, the Musical'. What a delightful play, with great lines and on behalf of our students, a great cast. I offered to help with ticket sales that night. Two years previous, Rick was knee deep in the co-directing of 'Beauty and the Beast' and it was that night that in retrospect I wonder was the beginning of his demise. As mentioned elsewhere, a major ten-minute sound glitch sent him into quiet paroxysms of angst until corrected. I am glad I helped out this year and there were no major glitches, but my presence accentuated my own thoughts around that time.

Saturday, December 8 was Christmas tree day for me with the help of some incredibly wonderful friends, but Saturday two years previous was the day Rick became seriously ill very suddenly, ending in death that night just before 10:00 pm. The hopeful, wonderful difference two years can make is in the loyal presence and support of friends who also knew this was the weekend. Carole, John and Russ accompanied me to find the best Christmas tree ever, cheer me on as I sawed (which was Rick's job) and they seemed to share almost as much joy as me. They caught on pretty quickly, however, that pointing out too many trees only added to my fussiness and time spent in the rain. The fun continued in my home once we got the tree inside and others joined us to help decorate and have chili. Rick would have shuddered at the attempts to assure the tree stood straight in its stand and the, oh so comical, "How many men does it take to put lights on the tree?" Apparently it takes five, with Ralph standing in the middle of my living room authoritatively pointing and directing how it should be done. There was some discussion from Russ about string 'tension', which caused me to puzzle out loud that I had only heard about that kind of tension in the context of knitting and crocheting. And then there was Patsy insisting that you start the lights at the top of the tree. *Say what?* Again, Rick would shudder at the calamity of wires not tactfully tucked in the branches as only he could do, but I have decided to love it the way it is. That Saturday, two years later, was made much more tolerable due to the love of friends.

Sunday, December 9

There are so many things we are learning to do well in our worship services and that Sunday was no exception. Rick would have been almost bursting at the seams with joy. We were reminded that morning in our 'dwelling in the word' exercise that two years ago that morning, everything stopped when people knew that Rick had died. Again, I have mentioned this elsewhere but that spontaneity and immediate response of acknowledgement and prayer is a milestone I had always hoped we would reach. Having grown up the first thirty years of my life attending church where we followed the same format or used the same prayer book every Sunday did not allow for church family to respond to and embrace the present as it unfolded. I had always believed that if order of worship needed to be abandoned to address an immediate need within a congregation, which included stopping and praying right at that moment, then it should be done. I am very thankful that my church family has come to a place where when vitally important or necessary, we can do so. But I digress.

We had lots of guests on that particular Sunday and there was spirit in the air. A vibrant praise team practiced, resulting in strong song leading of Christmas carols and a most wonderful newer song got us off to a most worshipful start. We were then treated to a terrifically crafted three-minute video where many of our children and teens enthusiastically recited verses from a passage, Philippians 2 from memory. Committing this passage to memory had been a project encouraged by a friend and one of our deacons, and seeing that video brought the Bible to life; it was exciting, and emphasized the importance of that chapter.

My friend Phyllis and I were 'done' for differing reasons. Such joy for me mixed with yet again, "Rick, are you seeing this? You were light years ahead on concepts of worship and not afraid of trying new things while being mindful that for some it would be a stretch. Well, dear man, today was one of those days and you would have loved every moment." What is also important to say about the video is two things: the boldness and joy with which those young folks cited Philippians 2, proclaiming a love for God. The video ended with that same deacon Martin reciting the entire passage himself. The zeal of our younger and older. What else touched me about this project came in the precious aside with another friend and quiet leader Lawrence, who could barely get the words out. He had wanted to act on this idea that came to fruition that morning since the summer when we as a congregation were encouraged to learn this passage. The fact that it finally came to be and as powerfully as it did caused him to have similar thoughts as mine around how much Rick would have enjoyed it and the entire morning. "God, you continue to remind us and show us ways for us to know and believe you are real. You instill faith and love in the hearts of all ages and that is exciting, wonderful, humbling and awesome. Thank you, Father, for continuing to come into our lives and walk alongside."

Sunday, December 9, 2012

A good day completed by Skyping with or talking to my two little families as they were decorating their own trees, and catching the last bit of the first *Home Alone*, where I therapeutically laughed until it hurt. *Gotta love that.*

December 11, 2012 –
Snap Dragons, Christmas Trees and Love

I didn't know what to expect this day that marks the end of year two without John Richard McBay (Rick Bear). As we have often pondered in our bereavement programs, sometimes the anticipation of the day is more difficult than the actual day and I have rediscovered that again personally.

Actually, it started the previous night with Brian's phone call, wanting to know how I was after my Christmas tree demise, which is a whole other story. My neighbour Floyd came to the rescue and helped me put it back securely into its stand. Brian was concerned because he understood how very special Christmas trees are for we McBays and he knew the amount of emotion behind this ritual. *Precious!* I still have my tree, and broken ornaments are just stuff.

My lifelong friend Debby called before 8:00 that morning, and I didn't even have to guess who was on the phone. Fifty-one plus years of friendship does that.

Laurena sent me a most lovely email and reminded me of the phone message she and Ralph received two years ago from her young nephew, offering support to them because he knew a good friend of theirs had died.

I had already planned to take the day off from Great Lakes but that was not meant to be, and that too was okay. Chief Administrator and dear friend, Don Rose, informed me that some time would be taken at the end of morning Chapel to remember Rick, so of course I went. While it must have been a little difficult for the new students of the past two years who never met Rick, they were patient, while several of our senior students shared memories of Mr. McBay. I was reminded in their words how much Rick impacted them, even when he could come across stern. They absolutely *knew* how much he believed in them. Then Mr. Rose announced that there would be a brief ceremony outside at Mr. McBay's memorial tree and stone at 12:10 pm.

So my plans for the day had changed again which was okay. I had enough time to purchase some white snap dragons for Rick Bear then treat myself to a bowl of coffee at our new, very innovative coffee/student drop in centre – Conversations. There I met my younger minister Dylan and we enjoyed each other's company and were then joined by Ron Kielstra, a most wonderful Great Lakes parent. Just enough time to get back to the school for a Christmas arrangement to be placed at Rick's tree and be surrounded by students and staff in prayer.

And speaking of Christmas trees, it dawned on me that the best thing I could take to the cemetery was a small potted tree and the white snap dragons. I was told the tree would be fine there for a couple of weeks and then I would bring it home to a more protected spot until spring arrived and then plant it somewhere on the property.

Brian, Shanna, Terral and Laura travelled down to meet me for supper at Cibo's in Grimsby. What a lovely way for us to mark this day together.

I have been surrounded by so much love and I am incredibly blessed. *Does it take away the hurt?* In some ways perhaps. *Is this getting any easier?* Sometimes I know it is. For anyone questioning how long this takes, let me know when it happens to you. I am still Mrs. Rick McBay, I am also Sandy McBay, Nana, and friend. The fact that Rick is feeling farther away is still unsettling and yet there have been so many ways he has felt near since he left December 11, 2010. Most recently, I felt Rick one morning when I looked outside to see that magical, gentle, snow globe shaker kind of snow falling while hearing 'Silent Night'.

I love you, Rick, a lot of people still desire to speak of and love you. Your life had meaning and I suspect it is mostly due to your desire to glorify God. Thank you.

"O love that will not let me go, I rest my weary soul in thee. I give thee back the life I owe, that in thine ocean depths its flow may richer, fuller be."
(Matheson, 1842)

Chapter 13

It's the Most Wonderful Time of the Year?

Two years of pondering, navigation, reality checks and life have become a book about how one important husband's death has changed his wife's life. It seems most natural to draw it to a close between Christmas and Rick's January birthday. Rick loved Christmas; we *his* family were into our third year without him, and while there was no magical difference the day after another December 11 or at Christmas 2012, there was a difference.

There is hesitancy in bringing this to a close in that it demands a letting go; it confirms a moving forward, and a fear that the meaning of who Rick was will be lost. I have mused several times the mystery and disbelief of it all. The lack of Rick's presence for 745 days and counting . . . and my knowing and loving him for thirty-eight years. And yet it is still wonderfully easy to talk about him with my family and friends, for which I am eternally thankful.

So this chapter is dedicated to how Christmas without Rick was seen through my eyes, those of my children and grandchildren.

We begin with Stuart Maclean. My friend Jo-Anne and I had front row seats at Stuart's Christmas show at Hamilton Place and Stuart did not let us or the packed house down. Two new Christmas stories sent his audience into guffaw laughter and his musical guest Reed Jamieson with the Vinylettes and John Sheard, gave new meaning to musical excellence and take your breath away beauty.

December 23 was our now annual Celebration of the Season evening service at church, which was instituted by Rick several years before. A glorious evening of song was woven into a more complete Christmas story from Old Testament references through to the rolling away of the Easter tomb stone. As ridiculously logical as it sounds, one cannot celebrate the gift of salvation from a saving son of God without rejoicing first in His birth. We had some wonderful young actors in our pre-teens and a junior choir who helped us 'Behold the Lamb of God'. Rick would have loved it. My grand-daughter Haley was most enthralled about Mary and the baby Jesus.

Christmas Eve and Christmas day, also my younger son Terral's thirty-first birthday, were a whirlwind of nonstop activity. Four grandchildren five and under gave their Nana the gift of seeing Christmas again through their eyes. All three nights a grandchild slept with me and Rick's place in bed was warmed again. There is nothing that can replace watching the pure innocence of children emanate in their sleep.

I had decided to create a short family devotional time for Christmas Eve since we had all attended church the night before. Remembering the birth of baby Jesus and remembering Papa with candles was something we could all participate in around the nativity made of olive wood purchased by Rick and me years ago from the Ten Thousand Villages Craft Sale.

Family Devotional

Christmas is about being happy that Baby Jesus was born. God loved all of us so very much that he sent his very special Son to earth to help us love each other.

That night we lit a candle to place at the nativity that Papa and Nana bought many years ago. Baby Jesus was in the middle because He was the most important and we lit our candle from His, which was the biggest candle, reminding us of His light and love.

Because Papa was not here with us and because Papa loved Christmas and Jesus so very much, Nana wanted to tell the family about his love for us. This was a request from Shanna, shortly after Rick died.

"Brian – Music put a spring into your Dad's step and heart. Any time you, Terral, and he played together reminded him of the value of being a Dad. The Christmas morning we unwrapped the CD, you and Terral created his heart was ready to burst. The fact that your life's work is music meant so much to him. He also loved working outdoors with you, splitting wood, making cider and playing catch on the side lawn.

"Terral – Music was not lost on you either. Teaching yourself to play guitar and using your music in worship is just so your Dad. But your natural ability to find your way around tools and anything hands-on is most definitely a gift from him and he loved you working alongside him. He was especially proud of you for getting your Masters while holding down a job, loving your family and being a part of your church.

"Shanna – Rick loved the fact that you played hockey; he loved that you were in the GL chorus; he loved when you shared in our adult conversations; he loved that you travelled to Zambia and was especially proud that you did so on your own; he loved that you became a nurse, and he loved having your wedding in the back yard.

"Laura – You and Rick knew how to have fun with each other and pull each other's chains in a fun way. The fact that you are a teacher told him you understand the value of education inside the classroom and out. He loved your determination and how well you and Terral fit together. He was also very impressed with your cooking and baking.

"Carter – Papa's first grandchild and first grandson. Papa was so excited when you were born. He loved having you with him in the back yard, riding in the wheelbarrow and on the riding lawnmower. A favourite memory he had was when you and he were sitting on the dock at the cottage and looking for fish in the lake.

"Leah – Papa's second grandchild and first granddaughter. We have many pictures of you and Papa in the backyard. He loved having you follow him around, playing with you in the sand, watching the campfire together and showing you things like making maple syrup. He loved how you walked with purpose and your dimples when you smiled.

"Haley – Papa knew how much you liked to cuddle and he loved doing that with you. He loved singing to you when you needed soothing and he especially loved listening to you chatter in your high chair. Probably Papa's favourite time with you is when we came to your Kindermusik class.

"Seth – The last picture of you and Papa is at your daddy's graduation. You were four months old. Papa would love to see what a big boy you are becoming and he would love how much you like Jake. He would also really love that you like to sing.

"It may be hard to remember Papa now so Nana lights her candle to thank him for his love and how much he taught me about loving Jesus.

"*Away in a manger, no crib for a bed*
The little Lord Jesus laid down his sweet head.
The stars in the bright sky looked down where he lay
The little Lord Jesus no crying he makes." **(McFarland, 1892)**

For the most part our family devotional went smoothly. It was more difficult for two-year-old Seth to understand what was going on, but he really liked lighting his candle. Carter and Leah seemed to especially like hearing what Papa loved about them.

Cookies for Santa, a carrot and dog food (at Leah's insistence) for the reindeer were left in the living room for Santa. 'Twas the Night Before Christmas' was read, four little lambs were snuggled into their beds and sleep for at least one did not come easy. My adult children brought all kinds of Rick Bear Christmas Eve snacks and we puzzled with a brand new Ravensburg 1000-piece puzzle they gave to me and couldn't wait to open. Nana didn't last as long as my kids.

In the twenty-nine Christmas's celebrated in this home, we have been lucky to have enjoyed maybe two of those with snow. We woke up that Christmas to a dusting of snow that brought the greatest joy to Terral, my Christmas child. Good choices of gifts were enjoyed all around and for the next two days, the four grandchildren played remarkably well for hours at a time with just a few squabbles in between. The distinctively different personalities of my four little ankle biters are something to behold I must say. There's no question that Nana's patience was tried on occasion and I don't like how that patience in me seems to be waning. There were a couple of times when all four tired children at once really pressed some buttons in me, but all in all, our time together was glorious.

I had promised a visit on Christmas Day to the wife of a senior friend from our church at a long-term care facility close by. When I told Eugene I would bring my family to visit Evelyn his immediate response was, "Will you sing?" A change in Evelyn's health dictated that a smaller group visit, so Brian, Terral and I decided to go. Delightfully, Carter and Haley came as well and I was very proud of them.

I remember visiting my grandfather many years ago as a child in a long-term care facility and being rather frightened. The kids were curious and great, we sang several carols and a couple of older hymns we knew Evelyn would enjoy. She even joined us on a couple of songs. We came away reminded yet again that there are a *lot* of people all over who are lonely, failing, perhaps abandoned by family, for whom a brief visit means so much. Merry Christmas, Evelyn and Eugene.

We had been outside in the biting wind to walk up and feed the horses up the road, and it was soon time to start packing things up so my families could get on the road before the first winter storm of the year really took hold. After a good family time together there is always that pocket of tension between leaving and getting back home to the more predictable structure young families need. Between Seth incessantly opening and closing Terral's musical Christmas/Birthday card spouting the Hallelujah chorus, *Hallelujah*, Leah finding all kinds of reasons not to eat her supper, *Hallelujah, Hallelujah*, Carter asking his daddy the same question repeatedly and Haley having a meltdown because Nana didn't line up the bottom of her leggings *Hallelujah, Hallelujah, Hallelujah*, I was about to have a meltdown of laughter and tears of my own. But would I trade a second of the insanity? The snuggles, the delightful giggles, the constant negotiating, the precious half-hour with my sons or the incredibly well thought out gifts by my daughters-in-law? *Hardly!*

Christmas 2012 was over. Rick was missed. Terral confided in me that he had gone to visit his Dad at the cemetery on Christmas Day. That touched me deeply. He must have done so during my brief nap while the turkey was cooking.

January 22, 2013. "Happy sixty-fifth birthday, Rick." Five people had acknowledged that with me already that day. You are still loved. On this day I would have taken you out for supper and you could have asked for the seniors' discount! Instead, I took Bri, Shanna, Terral and Laura to a wonderful Thai restaurant and we said Happy Birthday to you with green tea. I took the day off from Great Lakes and I am very thankful that I had that flexibility and wonderful support. Don brought me a plant basket and card.

Late January of that year, I contacted artist Holly Carr in Nova Scotia for some art related information. In 2007, I brought Holly to Grimsby for a large palliative education evening where she was 'the final act'. Holly paints on silk before her audience with music playing in the background. My son Brian played piano, and our volunteer program director at the time, Ev, read stories I had asked our volunteers to create about the very special relationships they had with their clients. It was an absolutely magical event.

Holly (who is Robert Bateman's daughter-in-law) is a very down to earth woman and I felt like we had personally connected very easily. When I emailed Holly that January, I told her about Rick's death and shared that I was moving forward in my search for the meaning behind it all. This was Holly's response, bless her heart:

"Looking for meaning in daily life can sometimes feel like a full-time profession, especially in some of January's gloomy days. I am continually amazed how the meaning and bliss can sparkle through even during the times when all you want to do is cry.

"Well, Rick Bear, there is a difference entering into this year three. It is definitely hope based, and that assurance goes a long way when I look at your picture and still ask how all this happened. Our trip to Alaska we never got to is now on the table for discussion for June 2014. Several friends have indicated interest (even Russ!) and Earl is ready to make that happen. I don't know what that will be like without you so I am counting on there being some undeniable level of your presence when I finally see whales, incredible ice bergs and enjoy some inland train travel. You are deeply loved."

Chapter 14

Who am I Now?

Revisiting this question ten years after answering it the first time – two daughters-in-law, four grandbabies and two years after Rick's death – is something I have tried to avoid. When I answered "Who Am I?" in 2003, life and I were very different. Rick and I were in a great place as husband and wife, our sons were beginning to pursue their dreams and relationships, and my life review revealed much for which to be thankful.

Our human document, who we are, is most definitely not static. As soon as we think we have answered that question, the very next breath we take changes us. However, I believe there are some life passages that leave some indelible marks. On December 10, 2010, if I had sat down to answer again, "Who Am I?" I believe there would have been many similarities to my answer written several years before. *Did Rick's death the following day really change me all that much?*

Sandra Elizabeth (Storen) McBay: *am I not still that person?* In some ways, most certainly. I still believe I am God breathed; I still melt at the sound of my sons' singing; I still look out for the underdog; I still love to laugh, and I still hate injustice. Spring is still my favourite time of year and I still believe there is much yet to do and be in my life. Loons at the cottage continue to give me hours of pleasure, my grandbabies are the most brilliant children on the planet and a great variety of musical pieces can send me to places of awe. Speaking out when I think it necessary has become a little easier, while tolerating meaningless conversations of fluff is much more challenging. But finding my way without Rick, as a single woman, mother and Nana, is changing me every moment.

I recently discovered some notes I had taken in a lecture years back featuring Dr. Therese Rando, Psychologist and author of several books about death, palliative care and grief. My respect for Dr. Rando is significant. She's brilliant; her vocabulary is light years ahead of mine, yet she presents with a wonderfully human and real nature. My notes reminded me of a statement Therese made about traumatic death in that "it takes longer to grasp reality". I don't know why I had forgotten that but reading that statement was most affirming. And in a world where experts throw around the word 'denial' so effortlessly, it was refreshing to have her suggest that denial may just be disbelief. There's that word again.

While rather shaky and uncertain at times, my premature single woman status is stabilizing, I *think*. That simple and often annoying 'passage of time' has carved a place of familiarity at least. I would much rather have Rick in my life, but I continue to take steps forward without him. The uncertainty still lurks within my internal compass. *Where am I going from here?*

Waking up February 27, 2013 to a flooded basement should have sent me into a complete tizzy but it did not. Yes, there were a couple of initial curse words upon discovery of floaties at the bottom of the stairs, but a meltdown demanded too much energy at a moment when immediate action was required.

What was ridiculously absurd about this mishap was that Rick did everything in his power to avoid the sump pump disaster. For a while, until he finally committed to a marine battery and back-up pump plan, he was almost consumed by what felt like imminent disaster each time it rained. It is only now, in his absence, having more recently acknowledged the need to restore the back-up system, that the main pump failed and I was pooched! I am reminded with every new person coming through my door with more renovation decisions for me to make, that having Rick here would make this new job a whole lot easier, and it would have been fun to make those decisions together. Right now, it's overwhelming but I try to remind myself that my insurance has got this, and I will be fine. As well, although I never saw myself being a contractor, and I know I use the term a bit tongue in cheek, I am pleased so far with how I have been working through this ridiculous upheaval. I never quite understood what all the drama could be about in a situation like this but I now understand the pressure of the multiple, time line decisions required and here I am as the solo decision maker. I am most confident that Rick would be proud, as am I. More importantly, it is just stuff.

Who then, am I now? I am still married to Rick and that won't change unless all the stars are aligned and the most incredible man enters my life. I have my doubts, but if that were ever to happen, it will be because it is supposed to.

I cannot imagine someone other than Rick but I also acknowledge the increasing loneliness. Often, I ask myself how someone my age, single and with similar values could exist out there let alone be interested in me. Yes, pitiful I know. But I do see with trepidation that there are some aspects of my life where I could become very set in my ways. Is that independence or is it the increasing age moulding me into someone I have always feared I would become?

Lately, I have been thinking a lot about Rick's mother Mary. His Dad – her husband Howard – died at the age of sixty-three, six months before we were married, and she lived without him until she was ninety. When I have challenges at home or become unwell, I think about how we responded to Mary when she experienced similar things. And I recall us not being the most present with her through some of those times. *How tragic is that?* It is those memories that cause me not to bother my kids when I am met with uncertainty, and yet I do confess there are times when that passivity backfires and I wish for more family interaction.

Elsewhere I have boasted a measure of resilience. Some look at me and can't imagine being in my shoes. I had similar thoughts of others before Rick died. At times I impress myself and my boys. Upon recent basement flooding, son Terral has been duly impressed with my composure.

And yet there is something else going on inside me that is difficult to name but frustrates to no end. Perhaps it's the antithesis to boasted resilience. Call it diminished confidence, a shaken foundation, uncertainty mixed with a desire to find a clearer path into my future. I know there is much yet to do with my life but I would kind of like to know what that may be. I can still spend literally hours in my living room at the end of a busy day or over a weekend and then chastise myself for the inactivity, the lack of purpose. The word unsettled comes to mind.

I confided in my friend Phyllis recently that my present existence seems to be one of concluding each day, "Well, I got through another one." *What kind of living is that?* The part of me that loved to stop and acknowledge awe-filled moments, take it all in, breathe the day, has not fully returned. I believe that part of me is still in there, but there is still much acclimatizing to this new life before *she* returns.

The principle of 'being' as opposed to busily 'doing' is something I preach often. Defining *me* by the busyness of my calendar and what I 'do' feels rather shallow. Perhaps this is why I am not comfortable in the cocktail party kind of conversation or in situations where folks need to posture and affirm their value by demonstrating how busy they are.

Instead of getting through another day, I look forward to the return of being in the moment, and there have been glimpses. Sunsets from my living room can be pretty spectacular and I have allowed a few to wash over me. During my time in Florida, relishing a morning walk in the soothing warmer weather, I witnessed for the first time a White Rainbow or Fog Bow. I couldn't wait to get back to my sister-in-law Marilyn's to tell her and her sister Jan about it. One afternoon while enjoying my second cup of coffee for the day, again from my living room, the glorious choral piece 'Chorus of the Hebrew Slaves' came on the radio and I was transported to a lovely place of calm.

Watching any of my four grandchildren is a lovely thing. I still don't fully understand the difference of that relationship. Rick and I loved Brian and Terral immensely and we so enjoyed watching them grow. But we were in charge; we needed to guide them the very best we could and the responsibility was staggering at times. With Carter, Leah, Haley and Seth my responsibility is second to their parents, granting a freedom to 'be' with them as Nana, which I couldn't enjoy as much when a parent. Just being allowed to watch them, witness their little minds turning at warp speed as their discoveries unfold and to be silly with them is a gift I don't take lightly. Plus, it's very cool when Laura tells me that Seth had a meltdown because he wanted to see Nana! *I'm a rock star!*

In September of this year I will get to share that rock star status with another grandchild from Terral and Laura. This is lovely news to share, especially for Terral and Laura. They were to have had child number three in March of 2013, but that little lamb's life ended just after the second trimester began. As the pregnancy was at the beginning of the second trimester, there remained a hesitation within me to celebrate, as I did not wish to see my kids go through that pain again. But who was I not to be filled with joy and hope when they were? And who was I to squelch Leah's joy around the fact that she was going to be a big sister and Seth was going to be a big brother? How's this for the complete joy and faith of a four-year old?

"Leah, did you know there's a baby in my tummy?"

". . . a real baby? Is it the baby that's in heaven?"

"Nope, it's a new baby."

"A *new* baby?! Daddy, Daddy, God gave us a new baby! God has the other baby in heaven with Papa, but he gave us a new one! *Yay!* Now I get to be a big sister again and Seth gets to be a big brother!"

A weekend had past with my family of eight coming to spend time with Nana and to help with decisions around my basement restoration had been good medicine. There are things in my life of which I am uncertain but loving my kids and grandchildren is not one of them. That infectious, unbridled, innocent joy on my grandbabies' faces when they see their Nana has almost miraculous qualities for the soul. Seeing anything through their eyes practically demands, at least in this Nana's eyes, that the world take notice. Yes, I guess I have arrived at being more obnoxiously vocal about these precious little lambs. Creating stories with all four of them on my lap or most spontaneously laying on the living room carpet to create indoor snow angels with Leah and Seth is what I vowed to do now that Papa is gone, and for many years to come I pray. The only down side, if there is such a thing, is that increasing back troubles and chronic pain greet me front and centre after every visit with my grandbabies. It is a very busy time and I refuse to limit my movements too drastically or I would miss out on so much, but I do pay for it the next day. And yet how could I have it any other way?

When they leave I am often overcome with sadness, especially on a Sunday. One look at Rick's picture and the tears are never far behind. But one of those moments when his presence became very real was my catching a ray of sun coming through the window. It landed on the photo I had created after Rick died, where his head was superimposed above me sitting on the couch with Carter, Leah, Haley and Seth. It was as if he were casting the light himself and pointing it right over the photo for me to see right at that second. We humans seem to need signs on occasion that everything is going to be all right. This was most definitely one that cloaked me in a moment of that deeper joy that can still be felt even when not all is quite right with the world. Again, Rick, thank you.

As far as desiring some direction for where I am going so to help me understand who I am now, I realize it is a tad presumptuous of me to just wait and see with the hope that God will zap me with a plan. *Do I not have some say in my future and am I not starting in some ways with a clean slate*? Yes, I must continue to support myself, which for now may be a bit restricting. But as I heard myself respond recently to a group of retired people who were lamenting how boring their life could be sometimes, there is just so much out there yet to do in this world. I will take that trip to Alaska; in fact, there is at least a dozen people already expressing interest to join me with a friend who plans such excursions.

My name is Sandra (Sandy) Elizabeth Storen McBay. Not by choice, I am single and am finally beginning to be reconciled to that fact. My love for God continues to unfold and He is still at work in me. My sons, daughters and grandchildren and I are finding our way, but Papa has not been forgotten. My character continues to be built (even in your absence Rick) and I am thankful for all that has passed my way. My life continues to have meaning, even in the wee hours of uncertainty, and strength is being renewed. *"Oh God you are my God, and I will ever praise You."* **(Beaker, 1991)**

Chapter 15

Moved by the Spirit

Included in this chapter are random thoughts as they unfolded over a two-year period. Random and stand-alone ideas, each recorded when the spirit moved me, that didn't seem to fit anywhere other than in this collection of short writings.

Eleven

What is it about the importance of numbers throughout our life trajectory? Birthdates, anniversaries, milestones, celebrations, tragedies, the time of birth or the time of death. For most of us I suspect, we have several numbers etched in our mind.

Over the years, May 10 has been very special, mostly, because that is my birthday. When I turned ten (double digits!) on the 10th, you would have thought I had been given the world. In fact, I had been banned by my mother from the basement at 332 Pinehurst in Oakville for two weeks prior because she was working on my tenth birthday present. Fortunately I did not succumb to the almost overwhelming temptations to peek and that lesson of patience has rewarded me many times over since. So, on May 10, 1964, I was finally able to open that forbidden door to discover a completely restored, red and white two-wheel bicycle (my first), complete with basket and bell on the front. Ten on the 10th was a very good day and still a vivid memory.

Of course there are *many* more such memories tied to important dates that continue to bring joy at recollection: my wedding day; the day our sons were born (Terral on Christmas Day like his Grandpa McBay); the first time I witnessed someone die – my father Frank Storen at 8:00 am on Sunday, February 7, 1988 and my mother Frieda Storen six months later at 1:30 am on September 6, 1988. Our sons' wedding days, the birth of our grandbabies and a plethora of other life passages all have numbers attached to them that are memorable.

Perhaps the most influential number to date is *eleven*. Our first son Brian was born September 11, 1981. Twenty five years later, the number 911 exploded around the world as we all witnessed far more than we would have liked in the terrorist attacks on Tuesday, September 11, 2001. Brian and I talked that morning and he somehow couldn't get past the fact that this had happened on his birthday, which caused him a bizarre question of responsibility. Years later, 911 has a whole additional meaning beyond the phone number to call in an emergency.

December 11, 2010 is with me every day; the day Rick died after we shared thirty-five and a half years of marriage together. While I do not experience sensations of dread or angst necessarily when I see, say or hear that number, it is now very different to me in all that it carries with it. I continue to measure my personal timeline and moving forward based on the number *eleven*. Each eleventh of the month is anticipated, confronted and left behind until the next one.

Ask anyone in a bereavement program about dates and times and you will hear similar reflections. So what is it about these numbers? Why do they bear such importance? I suspect it has something to do with a need to continue to place importance and meaning on the people we loved in the events with those numbers assigned to them.

Ridiculous Loneliness

From a spousal death perspective, ask any 'survivor' the number one challenge as they move forward and loneliness will be the resounding answer. Somewhere else in this writing I have touched on that but it keeps rearing its solitariness. October 28, 2012 and I had returned from a girls' weekend at a wonderful B&B in Hamlin, New York. The four of us had planned this time of rest, laughter, good food and mutual support a couple of months earlier.

Our time together fulfilled our expectations and more. We have been through a lot together as friends and the honesty shared was refreshing.

As we were driving home, the anticipated quiet and regret after a great time spent together became more evident. My sense of dread inherited from my mother Frieda started bubbling to the surface. When I dropped Phyllis off, I needed to ask John if we had come home to any bad news and thankfully we had not. *So what was it then?*

The cold, rainy weather influenced by the anticipated hurricane interestingly named Sandy had much to do with it. While coming home to an empty house is not new and most of the time I am used to it, this coming home felt harsher. I knew I would need to clean out the wood stove to get a fire going and I really looked forward to that wonderful warmth from my place of solace in the living room, but it all just felt so heavy. Fortunately my buddy Jake (he's a cat) didn't let me down when I walked in the door and he let me know I was missed.

But the friggin' loneliness after two days of closer proximity with good friends was a stark juxtaposition and easy to fall into. Rick continues to feel farther away, I continue to be disturbed by that natural progression, and licking my wounds seems to be a greater need at these times. Of course, he was not home for me to share the weekend with so I knew I would call both Brian and Terral. The heavy blanket of leaves across my entire back yard shouted of responsibility, which could not be addressed until after at least four more days of rain. And other than Jake, there was no one to share my lovely fire. Swear words! That loneliness becomes unspeakable, palpable, consuming and perhaps a little terrifying when I revisit the millionth time that this could be my life statistically for another twenty plus years.

Fortunately my greater sense of resilience kicked in and pushed me out the door to church where we and three other church congregations came together for a time of worship. The singing was great, our second minister Dylan's leading was purposeful and effective, and I visited with a few people at refreshment time. The most important interaction was with a friend named Fran whose husband died some years before. Fran attended my bereavement program. As only women whose husbands have died can, she has become a bit of a kindred spirit and she bears a strength that intrigues me. It is not harsh but it is a place for me that is still a little bit down the road, yet it speaks of promise.

Not new to many I am certain; loneliness is not restricted to being alone. Far more often since Rick died, I have found myself lonelier in the midst of groups or a crowd. Earlier in this process, there were many moments when I would feel almost incredulous as the people around me seemed quite content to carry on with life, apparently not aware that my world had been turned upside down. Did they not know my husband had died, did they not understand my brokenness? How dare they not stop their world since mine had been stopped? Although for many a very real part of grief, I am thankful I have moved beyond this "it's all about me" response.

Idle chit chat has never been a form of conversation in which I have enjoyed engaging. At the risk of sounding insulting, I wish not to give time to fluff. Life has always contained deep meaning for me, relationships have been about truth, investment and being courageous enough to be real with each other. I don't have time for fluff. Now more than ever, I find it difficult to place myself in the midst of 'cocktail conversations', to listen to someone whine about their mates, children, or disappointing benefit packages, and the like. Life's precious value and it's sometimes unexpected brevity has far greater meaning for me than whether or not I was made to wait in line too long at the bank or grocery store. It has been said that death has a way of levelling the playing field and I would rather have those on my team whose self-importance and attention to the minor has been replaced with giving attention to what and who really matters. If that alienates me from some, I'll have to get over that.

July 11, 2012 (19 months later)

As referenced earlier, the "Who Am I?" question is looming ever greater and presents itself from several provocations. When someone genuinely asks me how I am doing this long after Rick died, I stumble and fumble and search deeply for words. How I am seems dependent on many things: has it been a good and productive day; have I accomplished anything at all; am I okay with the fact that Rick is becoming more a place of memory than presence (a healthy necessity in grief), and am I okay with the fact that every new moment is now solo and who is this solo soul anyway?

Certainly, I have accomplished more outside this summer than last, much of it on my own with a healthy dose of pride. But in the next breath I look around and still ask, "Rick, why aren't you here enjoying this with me?" There is still a palpable void and sense of emptiness in most things that I do because they are no longer shared, and it's bloody lonely talking to Jake my cat about my day. However, Jake cuddles really well and is a delightful presence at the door when I return home each time. Ten years ago, I answered the question "Who Am I?" because I was asking the same of any new palliative volunteer I was training. It was refreshing to read my reflections again recently, but I am still not sure how I would answer that now. The confidence then that took me fifty-three years to build is not as strong since Rick died. And yet in other ways, my voice is becoming stronger. Certainly the assignment is an ongoing one as each new day alters our lives and life view. But I am significantly different now, and again, language which I so enjoy, evades me.

One of my bereavement program co-facilitators continues to describe himself many years after the death of his wife as married. When I first heard John say this two and three years into his 'new life', I wondered about that. But Rick was still very much alive at the time and I simply could not identify. I get it now, John. I too am still married to Rick. I still wear the rings he gave me, I use the vanity license plate 'RICK BR', I bought him years ago. I continue to negotiate all that is involved in living on the rather labour intensive property where we brought up our boys and our grandbabies love to explore. Perhaps the strangest contradiction I still feel is each night when I go to bed and the following morning when I awake. It is the same bed, I still sleep on 'my side' but it is still foreign that Rick is not there. Not long ago I tried again to sleep on his side. The first attempt was quite uncomfortable, however, sleep came easy on his side for about a week. I am back to my side again as it is closer to the bathroom. Often, I find myself asking even now, "Rick, where did you go?" Perhaps this is the greatest difference between sudden death and death from a protracted 24/7 illness. Disbelief maybe just takes a lot longer to dissipate because we just didn't see it coming.

Dream, July 23, 2012

While I continue not to put a whole lot of stock in dreams they are, at the same time, fascinating and do have a foundation of reality to them.

It had been, mostly a blissfully chaotic weekend at my sister's cottage on Adams Lake, which is now their home. For over thirty years our family had enjoyed the rest and solace of this little piece of heaven each summer and a few times in the winters. Many family building and affirming memories are nestled among the trees with the call of the loon. Rick is still everywhere at the cottage for me, which is wonderful and soul sucking all at once.

This was the first time my two little families and I were together in Rick's absence with Dawn and Doug and we were to be with my nephew Cameron, his wife Kathleen and daughter Alana. On my way to the cottage I got a call from my sister to report that the twins Cam and Kathleen were expecting in September had arrived six weeks early. Certainly the complexion of the weekend changed dramatically. Cam was able to join us with Alana and his twin nephews for a few hours. At one point there were seven children under the age of five and ten adults. Amazing how quickly after the fact you forget the chaos and remember only the wonderful and there was lots of wonderful.

My families left Sunday night and I had to retreat to the dock with my tears. We had a delightful three days together but again, Rick's absence was strong. I awoke early the next morning from a very busy dream and it felt important enough to get up and record on paper before my foggy brain lost it. The recording of this dream includes small details which to any reader may seem inconsequential but are, for me, important pieces of the story.

The core of the dream was based around my desire to take in the summer clearance sales at Mark's Work Warehouse. But I was not at the store in Perth, I was back in Grimsby. I was in a frantic search for matching proper sized items on sale. Bringing my own shopping bags somehow got confused with theirs. Four chosen items changed to five with a free one being added. But I still wanted a blue, yellow, green and white striped top that illusively haunted me. In a conversation during the purchase transaction the sales lady, my senior by a few years, somehow got onto the topic of loved ones dying. I told her about Rick and she told me about her adult daughter. A tender moment between strangers. But I needed to find that striped top so I decided to walk to Vineland (approximately twenty kilometers) to a Mark's store that doesn't actually exist there. No success and it was closing time so I decided I should start walking back when I remembered it was Wednesday night, mid-week Bible Study and I needed to let Rick know I was going to be late. But for whatever reason I could not initiate that phone call, so I called my friend Ralph to ask if he could pick me up in time for church. Ralph had other plans, (which is so not Ralph) but he assured me he would pick me up.

My son Terral appeared out of nowhere and there were still several shoppers milling around. I told him I couldn't understand why Ralph was so late and that Dad would be waiting for me at church. A commotion to the right of us identified a female police officer and a crowd of 'volunteers' approaching, a most determined look on the officer's face. She informed me she was tempted to place me under arrest for causing so much worry as to my whereabouts. Someone had called in reporting my disappearance and there were search parties covering a thirty-kilometer radius "as we speak", hence the number of men, women and children accompanying her. Devastation and embarrassment caused me to blurt out, "I'm sorry, I just wanted to find something to wear to help me feel pretty again!"

The last part of the dream I recall was Terral and I encountering a young boy on our way back home who looked lost and disheveled. He had escaped some terrible scenario that was responsible for him not seeing his parents for five years. As dreams tend to do, we then encountered the father who had never stopped looking for his son and assured him his son was safe. Abrupt end of dream and I woke up to a ferocious headache and a slight return of vertigo.

Why do we have such bizarre dreams? Rick was in the picture but never visible. Do I take from that that I am progressing in William Worden's fourth task of relocating the deceased to a place of memory? But I still wanted him there, in the dream and when I woke up.

September 2012 –
Four Weddings and at Least One Funeral

From July 15 through September 22, I have attended, without Rick, four weddings and a funeral. While I was touched and honoured to be invited to the first three weddings of Rick's past students and chorus members, the thought of attending those without him was so very odd and a tad frightening. Upon accepting the invitations, I gently let the three couples know that I would quietly slip out once the dances began and they were most respectful. All three were wonderful events although going solo, even in a crowd of folks most of whom I knew, is not something I handle well. Perhaps my awkwardness was noticeable to no one but myself, I don't know, but there were several moments in each that I wished for magical powers to simply disappear.

Friday, September 7, a distressing phone call came in just after 9:00 pm. My dear friend Phyllis was crying and informed me that one of our friends from church had died very suddenly at home a few hours before. I asked her if she wanted me to come over. Quickly I changed out of my nightgown and got to her and John's place. Reportedly, our friend Gord was outside preparing for a moose hunting trip with his son Leith. His wife Linda called him in to supper and when he didn't respond she went looking for him. Linda found Gord on the ground by the car and at that second her life changed forever. She immediately began CPR, and somehow found a way to call a friend who arrived quickly. Gord was dead. Linda had her friend call Tallmans, our collective funeral director family, friends and fellow faith followers.

A home death requires police intervention and investigation as well as a visit from the coroner. My first desire was to drive over to be with Linda, having a pretty good idea of what she was beginning to encounter with this sudden, most unexpected death. But I knew she was in good hands with the Tallmans and I also surmised I would just be in the way. Sunday morning I made a point of dropping off some of my home-grown sunflowers and a card inviting Linda to call me during those future moments when she will just want to scream and need someone to listen. I also pledged to check in with her regularly.

Because we are part of a Christian fellowship, which uses only our God-given instruments of voice to worship musically, four of us were asked to form a quartet to lead singing during the funeral service and present one of Gord's favourite hymns, 'How Great Thou Art'. We were slated to sing after Gord's two daughters Kendra and Patti spoke about their Dad, which cast a foreboding apprehension upon the four of us. It always astounds me how we are able to draw upon unknown strength in such emotional situations to do what we need to do and do it well. For the record, I believe the unknown strength is that of the spirit within us. When we sat down, our soprano Eartha burst into tears, echoing what we all felt. Gord was honoured well that day and I need to make a point of checking in with his wife Linda on a regular basis as several did for me.

September 22, 2012, my nephew Stephen married his bride Alli in Ottawa. They asked their three aunts to give a reading during the ceremony and I was most honoured to read an excerpt by Ann Morrow from 'By the Sea'. Wonderful craftsmanship of words gives me great joy and I looked forward to delivering well their sentiments through Ann's words.

As the church was filling up and the time drew closer for the ceremony to begin, I became overwhelmed by surging emotion. My brother was here from British Columbia, my sons and daughters-in-law were present, and this was a wonderful family event. I turned to Steve's Aunt Trudy and said, "Trudy, I am barely holding it together at the moment." On the spot, Trudy leaned over the pew, touched my shoulder and prayed right then and there on my behalf. For someone who believes in acting spontaneously, even in the orchestration of a formal moment, this loving act was perfect and my reading went well. However, the emotion of this family celebration was never far from the surface, and as people followed Steve and Alli out of the church building, I blurted to my brother Brian, "I have to get out of here *now*." We exited a side door into a large, fortunately empty room where I found a chair and created a small place of temporary refuge. Brian asked if I wanted him to stay or to give me a couple of minutes to which I responded the latter. Moments later, I heard a door open and footsteps across the floor to where I was sitting and looked up. There was my handsome younger son Terral in his blue suit motioning for me to stand up, and I fell into his arms and sobbed. Gotta love your children when they find the best way possible at times to support and show their love. Our roles reversed for a few moments.

Another couple of significant notches on my belt entitled 'My New Life' are indelibly engraved and I carry on.

Chapter 16

I'm Told I Am Not Finished Yet

This chapter was written around the time of our thirty-eighth wedding anniversary.

Chris Irwin, a Producer of CBC Sports, wrote to me to express that he was moved by my story. I was astounded. We met over the phone on the morning of Remembrance Day when Rick and I were listening to Stuart Maclean's Vinyl Café radio program. We McBays are big fans and have all attended at least one of his Christmas shows. This particular show Stuart of course devoted to Remembrance Day. Instead of one of his own stories about Dave and Morley, he gave full attention to a story written by this young man Chris Irwin, a CBC colleague. Chris wrote about the time that he and his brother and family made the pilgrimage to Vimy Ridge with his WWII veteran father. Chris wanted to play his bagpipes for his father at Vimy and the tale that unfolded was quite incredible and deeply emotional. It reminded me of my father, the fact that he had been a prisoner of war in Barth, Germany, for over a year and it also reminded me of two of my uncles who honourably fought for their country and the freedom of others.

I was a blubbering ninny by the time Stuart finished reading the story and I listened very carefully for the name of its author. When Stuart announced the story had been written by Chris Irwin from Burlington, the rapid and intense search at the computer began. I found a C. Irwin on Canada 411 and immediately made a call. The words that stumbled out of my mouth when his wife Ellen answered were something like: "Is this the home of Chris Irwin, whose story was just read on Stuart Maclean's Vinyl Café?" Ellen hesitantly said yes, so I ploughed on: "My name is Sandy, I feel like I am stalking you for which I apologize. I am calling from the Niagara area and I just had to talk to Chris and invite him to come and speak at the school where I work. You see, my father fought in the same war; he was a prisoner for over a year and I think Chris's story needs to be heard, especially by our teens at Great Lakes Christian High School."

Chris came on the phone and I apologized again for stalking him and his family, but the result was that he agreed to be our guest speaker and bagpipe player at our Community Supper. He brought his entire family and it was delightful. To say that we have continued a friendship since then would be an embellishment but Chris and I have kept occasional email contact. He has welcomed this book to be read during down times. *Wow!* The word humbling comes to mind.

But back to the reason for this additional chapter . . .

A good friend Ev, told me that she believed I was not finished with my story. She said she felt there was more to hear, but she didn't expand. Ev has helped with the One Step at a Time bereavement support program for many years now. Her husband Don died some years ago, which she wrote about for this book. We have 'done our personal grief' so very differently but we have been able to support each other well. She is one of the 'Single Rose' women whose husbands have died and we share dinner together regularly at a favourite pub, the Judge and Jester. Perhaps because of our history of working together for over fifteen years and now walking alongside each other in grief, Ev had observed some things about me during the third year, which she believes I needed to put in words.

Well, with very mixed feelings, I acknowledge that I am okay on my own. I still don't like it and I find myself wondering when I look at Rick's picture how we possibly loved each other for almost forty years. He feels so very distant now and that saddens me deeply. I am fulfilling the prophecy I have lovingly offered so many, that the gap between meltdowns is widening and their intensity is lessening – most of the time. Any new experience without Rick brings tears, especially tender moments with my two little families.

May 31, 2013 was our thirty-eighth wedding anniversary and yes, I am still married to Rick. It felt important to acknowledge that on Facebook which I include here:

May 31, 2013 – Facebook Entry

Thirty-eight years ago today, Rick Bear and I were married. It was an equally hot and muggy day. His mother Mary had so wanted her then six grandsons and family to play a game of baseball since we already had a built in team. Mind you, two or three of the grandsons were barely old enough. We didn't end up doing that but May 31, 1975 was a good day.

I think the Bear would be pleased that I planted the butternut squash yesterday and that I got out this morning at 7:00 am to plant three varieties of tomatoes. While I was not quite as anal as he in getting the string out to make sure the rows are straight, I did keep my eye on the first plant as my guide.

I think he would be proud of me for handling the past three months of saga around a flooded basement and the six-week restoration and insurance aftermath. And I am pretty sure he would have a twinkle in his eye around the fact that I sought out the CEO of our insurance company around the most recent car accident (*not my fault!*) comedy of errors and reimbursement *frustrations!*

I know Rick would be tickled with how our four grandbabies are faring and that a fifth is on the way. In fact, Carter and Haley are coming for a two-night sleep over with Nana tonight. Uncle Terral will be with us for supper as he acknowledges this day with his Mom. And I know without a doubt that the Bear would love how our sons are finding their way through life with great wives, delightfully unique children and interesting jobs. There are so many moments I am deeply saddened that he is not here to witness all of this. Last weekend, I got to hear my boys sing at a most wonderful, Street Porch Party in Kitchener. Yes, I am their mother but *they really are good.* Happy Anniversary, Bear.

*

Babysitting Carter and Haley for not one but two nights was a first for me. This may not seem like a big deal to many but it was for me. They were terrific; we were busy and our time together was delightful, in spite of my uncertainty – again, without Rick. And yes, there were a couple of times when tears were at the ready over precious moments. A campfire with marshmallows had been promised but the weather did not cooperate.

141

Nana got a bit creative and we roasted marshmallows in the living room over candles instead. It was quite a hit.

Managing my yard has demanded much and it feels like I have just skimmed the surface, yet to others it looks beautiful. I was able to host our church youth group and all they noticed was an awesome campfire over which they roasted hotdogs, marshmallows and made Smores.

When Rick and I bought our home twenty-five years ago we had determined to host many such events over the years and we did. I think he would have smiled over this most recent one.

I guess when I look back to December 11, 2010, and then fast forward to now, I can say with a confidence, which is less shaky, that I am okay. Rick's death, its consequences for my life and the fact that in the same breath I can miss him so deeply while wondering how foreign it feels at times that I knew him for forty years, is still a mystery to me. During a recent adult Bible class, my pastor Noel asked everyone to name someone they were looking forward to seeing in heaven. I could barely speak and almost whispered, "My husband." I couldn't even say Rick's name.

A deeper wisdom of life accompanies me now. I have no time for lame conversations and speaking up when I feel it is important or necessary has become an integral part of who I am.

A couple of interesting moments occurred prior to my car accident on May 10, 2013 – my birthday. A couple of days before, I met with our financial advisor Roger to re-visit my financial status and to ask if I could afford to send Brian and Terral a small gift of money to help them with a couple of things. The morning I headed for my sister's cottage in the Perth area, I put two envelopes with cheques in the mail and thought at the time, *Well, if something happens, they will receive this.*

Two days later, as I was heading to my nephew's home outside of Ottawa, I decided to have a chat with God that went something like this: "Okay, God, I am not sure about this praying for travelling safety thing but I appreciate that I have got this far. I am asking you to keep me safe in the rest of my travels. I have a lot of living yet to do, two great families, four awesome grandbabies with a fifth on the way, and I wish to live long enough to see them grow." A few hours later, my lovely little blue car was hit from behind, my sister and I were sent into a relatively deep, marshy ditch along the side of the highway. Not a scratch or broken bone for either of us, but a totalled car. "Thank you, God."

And, as reported in my Facebook post, after two weeks of ridiculous frustration with my insurance company who I am sure at this point flinch when they see my name on their call display, I graciously but purposefully sought out the CEO of said company and then things finally fell into place. Two weeks later, I received a gift card in the mail from said insurance company thanking me for my patience.

July, 2013

God continues to work in puzzling and mysterious ways within me. My week of holidays with my sister Dawn and brother-in-law Doug in Perth, a little piece of heaven for the past forty years was 'full of opportunities'. Doug had hurt his leg quite badly and required lots of doctor visits, care and attention. I arrived on the Friday of a most momentous storm back in the Niagara Peninsula. My son Brian called the next morning because he had something to tell me about my house. I screamed "Noooooooo!" right away because I knew my basement flooded again, not three months after the repairs from the first flood. This time, five inches of rain in three hours, and six hours without hydro were the culprits.

Copious time on hold with the insurance company before being able to make a claim, many more phone calls and emails over the week consumed a lot of my dock time with the loons. But on the positive side, I sent an email out to five people at home – "SANDY NEEDS YOUR HELP!" and within an hour, three friends were in my basement with wet vacs and my time on hold with the insurance company paid off, because a restoration company showed up while they were still there. As well, my neighbours Floyd and Carolyn were troopers while I was away. They too were flooded and we commiserate but move forward together.

Southern Ontario had been socked with wicked storms that summer and insurance companies were working round the clock to meet our needs as well as those in Toronto and Calgary, Alberta. It had been most depressing to come home to a torn up basement again, but I learned some important things towards ongoing negotiations that time around.

Thursday of that week away, I was finally able to connect with my family doc Seamus, as I had been waiting on results from a mammogram breast biopsy from two weeks prior. The diagnosis was ductal carcinoma in situ, thankfully the earliest form of breast cancer, which I was told is non-invasive, non-life threatening and treatable by surgery and radiation. Well crap, I didn't need to hear that.

But because I instinctively knew something was up after the second call back, because I had time to begin to acknowledge the possibility, and because it seemed like a 'good' cancer, I was feeling mostly at peace. Granted I didn't relish being in hospital even for one night and I confess the 'c' word does rattle one's foundation, but as I said to God less than two months previous, I still have a lot of living to do and I plan to do just that.

God's mystery in all this unfolded more specifically from a televised church worship program. Televised worship has been very suspect for me over the years but some good friends recommended this one out of The Chapel in Lockport, NY. The pastor, Gerry Gillis, speaks for at least forty minutes with no notes and ties life lessons with scripture creatively and with not over the top animation. Today's lesson entitled 'Grow Up' focused on the first few verses from James 1: "Consider it pure joy, my brothers, whenever you face trials of many kinds, because you know that the testing of your faith develops perseverance. Perseverance must finish its works so that you may be mature and complete, not lacking anything." **(James, 1)**

Hmmm, the first time those words were brought very specifically to my attention was when I met with a counsellor years ago as I was struggling in my marriage. I did *not* wish to hear those words. Thankfully, the counselling paid off and Rick and I saw twenty-five and half more years together with lots of joyful times.

No, I don't believe at all that this scripture is telling me or anyone else that I need to take a stance of jumping for joy when stuff happens in our lives. And I don't believe that God somehow brings that stuff and watches to see if we are strong enough to handle it. But I do think the Creator of all things works my faith and perseverance through it all. And if I am willing to let it unfold as it needs to, maturity is coming through perseverance and perseverance is coming through the adversity or 'stuff'. Again, Rick got this well before I did. There is greater clarity now around his often annoying building character philosophy. "I get it, Bear."

Well, somehow the stars aligned, or God arranged for me to see His goodness, and a number of amazing things unfolded over the following month. When Seamus suggested I go locally for surgery and to Hamilton for follow up radiation, I was glad he also gave me a day to think about that. I had reservations for reasons I will keep to myself. I knew I needed to run that by Laurena before she and Ralph headed out for Europe the next day. Her immediate response was to suggest I request a referral to a surgeon in St. Catharines and work out of the brand new hospital. Because I knew of this surgeon, I ran it by Seamus and within twenty-four hours I had received an appointment to see her two weeks later.

Meanwhile, my sister Dawn went immediately into nurse mode and wanted to find out as much information and resources as possible for me. One of those resources just happened to be the recently retired head of the Juravinski Cancer Centre in Hamilton, who is a friend of the family. A week later, I received a call from this gentle spoken man who answered all my questions and assured me I would be in very good hands with the surgeon in St. Catharines. While I so appreciated the benefit of being connected to experts based on a friend knowing a friend, I was deeply struck by the fact that literally thousands of other people receiving diagnoses of cancer or other serious illnesses every day do not enjoy those connections. And that is wrong.

Another nurse friend, Linda, accompanied me to my appointment with the surgeon for which I was thankful. Dr. Anna Kobylecky spent over an hour with me, which felt unheard of to me. This was further emphasized when we exited her office to a waiting room of people lined up outside the door and I was extremely humbled. Stage One cancer threw me a bit because I originally understood this ductal carcinoma in situ was contained. I was informed I would receive a surgery date within seven to ten days, to occur over the following four to six weeks.

Those who know me understand the importance I place on how things happen for a reason. Upon return from my visit with Dr. Kobylecky, I had just sat down in the living room to begin digesting all the take home information when one of the most incredible pieces of music came on CBC. 'Spiegel im Spiegel' or, 'Mirror in the Mirror' is a gently gorgeous piece with piano and violin, which was used in a movie called *Wit*, that I use in my palliative teaching. A particular scene in the movie is beautifully and emotionally touching. The first time I saw it I blubbered like a fool. Having viewed this movie well over twenty times now, I am still moved. I stop in my tracks whenever I hear that piece of music.

Then time stood still. After waiting a week to hear a surgery date, I called the office and I was asked to call back two days later. I did on the Friday and was asked to call again the following Tuesday. The frustration level was escalating because we were approaching the beginning of another school year at Great Lakes, and I was scheduled to begin teaching another palliative volunteer course mid-September as well as start another bereavement support program. Most importantly, McBaby #5 was due in a couple of weeks from Laura and Terral. Many ducks to align in a row.

It's not every day that one receives a phone call at 9:30 on a Sunday night from a surgeon. Dr. Kobylecky wanted to know if I would be willing to take advantage of an O.R opening two days later. I stumbled and sputtered a bit and immediately said yes. Pre-op was arranged the very next day, son Brian came down that night and we left my home at 6:00 am the following morning for this brand new hospital. As we were driving, I was hopefully watching the scenery for a flock of geese to fly by. Two V formations of these birds played a most important role the day Rick died. I was disappointed not to see any as we were passing Lake Ontario. But yes, not one but two formations flew across just as we were entering the hospital parking lot and I shouted with joy. I was going to be fine.

Surgery prep was uncomfortably not fun, but then Brian was able to come back and stay with me until I was taken to the O.R. I had bugged him more than a couple of times to find out how he could play the gorgeous grand piano downstairs in the front lobby of the hospital, then I let it go.

When I awoke at 2:20 back in day surgery, Brian was able to rejoin me and he reported he had been able to play the piano for probably about twenty minutes. Even though I didn't get to hear that, I was thrilled because he is good, it was such a wonderful thing for him to be able to do, and I think he told me in my post-surgery fog that he had even received a couple of requests. Here is the list he remembers playing – all without sheet music:

My Task

Had A Busy Day

Smiling Through (those three taught to him by a ninety-year-old client he worked with)

Loch Lomond

Amazing Grace

He Leadeth Me

Be Still My Soul

What A Wonderful World

When I Grow Too Old To Dream

Terral and the rest of my family thoroughly enjoyed Brian's email updates throughout the day and were particularly entertained by my vain attempts to text people from Brian's phone and email later from Laurena's iPad. *Give me a keyboard please, this texting and touch screens are crazy.* Probably the best email I received was from my cousin Judy, who has had breast cancer twice and whose sister Carol has also been a survivor. Simply written: "Cancer picked on another Storen (my maiden name) . . . big mistake!"

So many things had occurred in 2013. But to those reading this who may be in the early months or years of grief, please hear me: If you allow yourself to *just be* in your experience, if you allow those who care to support you, and if you can find a reason to allow God to walk alongside you, no matter how much some of you may have felt abandoned in the past, *you will be okay!*

And yep, I will be okay, but I still rather Rick were here.

Thanks for listening.

Conclusion

I have always identified with Mary, the mother of Jesus who was said to "ponder all these things in her heart". To those who have stayed to the end of these, my ponderings, I thank you. Giving meaning to who Rick was, how he is deeply missed, what was unique about him and how he impacted many for the better has been at the core of this literary response to my grief. For now at least, it feels like I have come to a natural ending and the catharsis has been a most wonderful contribution to my ongoing healing.

Walking alongside others, hundreds who I did not know until they had a need, has become a most natural part of who I am. Some have said I have a gift. I thank them for that observation and I thank my Creator for the giving of said gift. I would much rather sit and be with someone at end of life, in bereavement support to hear their rich stories, or enjoy meaningful conversations with family and friends most dear, than engage in light conversation on matters not of the heart.

We all have very different ways of grieving, expressing and sharing that grief; moving through it, denying it and finally reconciling to it. Sometimes we forget that; however, despite what the theorists theorize, there is no script for grief. It will be all consuming for several seasons perhaps, and its complexion will change with each approaching season. While I suspect it will be spring for me, I can say with confidence that whether, summer, fall or winter, we will wake up one day and conclude we are going to be okay, deep joy is returning to our lives, we have conquered what may have seemed unconquerable along the way, and there is still much of life to be lived. When that day arrives for the person reading this, celebrate that. Go out and *breathe the day.*

If these words from one who continues to discover how to help others at end of life and in bereavement, help those much newer in their grief, Rick's death will have provided some semblance of purpose, although most uninvited to we who loved him.

I dedicate these two plus years of thoughts to my young families and a couple of others:

Brian who gently steps into peoples' lives with his music therapy and reminds them they are of value;

Shanna who conscientiously helps young parents as a labour and delivery nurse;

Carter – Rick's and my first grandchild, whose joy for life is manifested in his infectious giggles; and Haley who loves to cuddle and have a very tactile connection;

Terral, who speaks truth, loves life and inherited his Dad's sense of 'fixing';

Laura who teaches Grade 1 children 'they can' and is very creative;

Leah whose little strut in her walk struck at the very core of Papa's heart; and Seth, whose determination and impish smile strikes at the very core of Nana's heart.

My friend Debby also learned far too soon about grief through the chronologically flawed and most personal death of her daughter Carey Lee. Neither of us can truly identify with each other's loss but we have a history that has seen us through several other life challenges and listening is easy.

"Rick Bear, I continue to miss you every moment. From the movie 'The Life of Pi' I echo these words: 'I suppose in the end, the whole of life is an act of letting go, but what always hurts the most is not taking a moment to say goodbye. I was never able to say thank you.' So, thank you, dear man, for loving me, especially when it was hard. Thank you for our sons. Thank you for never giving up, on us, life, the challenges you called opportunities, and your love of God. Many others would."

Finally, two poems whose meaning continue to provide me solace:

If You Stand Very Still

If you stand very still in the heat of a wood
You will hear many wonderful things;
The snap of a twig and the wind in the trees,
And the whirr of invisible wings.

If you stand very still and hold to your faith
You will get all the help that you ask;
You will draw from the silence
the things that you need,
Hope and courage and strength for your task

Written by <u>Winifred Emma May</u>

A Good Friend

A good friend will always give you the better of two choices.

Will hold your hand when you are scared.

Will help fight off those who try to take advantage of you.

Thinks of you at times when you aren't around.
Helps to put the past behind you.
And understands when you need to hold on to it a little longer.
A good friend helps you to become a better person.
Smiles for you when they are sad.
Understands your worst mistakes.
And is loving you unconditionally.
No matter where we go, or who we become,
never forget who helped us get there.
*Written by Carey Lee Lytle – some wisdom she
learned in her too short thirty-two years.*

Epilogue
August 16th, 2015

It felt necessary to include an epilogue of sorts at the time of publishing "Twelve Weeks of Winter and Beyond", as much has unfolded in two years. One of my desires for this book was to provide hope to those much fresher in their grief, especially those whose loved one died suddenly. I believe in hope, have witnessed its accomplishments many times in my life and others. Hope, an unseen mystery, reminds us that there is always something going on in the bigger picture that will see us through, regardless of the circumstance. Hope sustains and gives us energy to look forward to another day.

In palliative care, often I heard the rather judgemental observation of someone at end of life that they should not be given 'false' hope. Most often that declaration has been made by the observer who has not been in those shoes personally. Again, if hope gets us up in the morning to breathe one more day, let us never rob someone of that. But I digress.

Two years ago I was travelling another area of uncharted territory, that of cancer diagnosis, surgeries, and multiple discussions of treatment plans. Not all was pleasant over 18 months, 60 plus hospital visits, radiation and chemo. And, I wish never to be prescribed Dexamethasone ever again. However, the pluses were many. After 25 radiation treatments and my first time in the chemo chair, I decided very quickly that I needed to do something positive with this experience. An email to the acting CEO of the hospital at the time, Sue Matthews who was also going through breast cancer treatments resulted in a visit from her during one of my chemos. I had commended to her all the staff with whom I had contact so far. Our conversation focused around good patient care and how hospitals were finding innovative ways to do just that. I had become aware of the Kingston, Ontario General Hospital and its very high credibility rating due to involving patients and their families in all aspects of their hospital programs. Sue was much more aware of this than I, and we had a great conversation about something called the Patient Family Advisory Council.

After expressing my appreciation to the Walker Family Cancer Centre for exemplary care over 18 months I was approached by them to consider co-chairing a similar yet brand-new Patient Family Advisory Council for the centre. It was not difficult to agree: a structured, hospital sanctioned venue for patients and their families to give constructive feedback on their care, to identify areas of improvement, and to affirm measures of care that are working well is a perfect way of giving greater meaning to my own experience and such a great demonstration of a health care field that is listening! After purposeful public promotion of this new council, my co-chair and I have 45 interested people to interview. Clearly, we have touched a nerve in a most positive way.

A couple of weeks ago, upon return to work from two of the above mentioned interviews I experienced a new sensation, one of excitement for my future and a renewed sense of purpose. Good coming out of challenge should not continue to surprise me, but it does. It always renews in me that illusive phenomenon mentioned earlier called hope. And, RickBear would be pleased.

One year ago I moved from our home of 26 years. With the help from my sons and a lot of community, the transition was quite smooth. There are many things I miss about that lovely home – backyard campfires, the vegetable garden, our little 'hosta hollow', the riding lawn mower and the fact that it was 'our' home. But I don't miss a sixty foot driveway full of snow in prevailing winds or worrying about sump pumps. My new home fits me nicely and has enough room to welcome my grandbabies for sleepovers.

One thousand, six hundred and ninety-eight days later, I am embracing life and I know with certainty that those much fresher in their grief will be able to do the same.

Thank you

While I understand the term 'acknowledgements' for a book, I have chosen to be more simplistic and list several 'thank yous' instead. And yet, as most people who have been the recipient of help and support great or small know, the phrase just isn't enough.

How do you properly thank people who have consciously stepped into a limping soul's circumstances to walk alongside and make a difference big or small? How do you appreciate well, the loving help so freely given and sometimes difficult to receive? Simple words of appreciation for life saving and sustaining acts of kindness.

This is my best shot . . .

Harry van Bommel – thank you, Harry, for encouraging me to continue this project, for proof reading and citing helpful suggestions and for graciously picking up from where we left off each time we re-enter each other's lives.

Chris Irwin – a kindred story writer, a believer in humanity, a gentle but strong soul.

Seamus Donaghy – my most favourite Doc in the world, and his wife Mary, who continue to respect and support my journey as well as take care of my unexpected physical responses to Rick's death.

Laurena Tallman – who encouraged me to finish this and who continues to care about me on many levels.

Those willing to share their stories – Ev, Iris, Laurena, Anne, Pat, Kirstin and Elsje.

Kathleen – for patiently answering everything computer because Rick is no longer here.

My artist neighbour and friend – Floyd Elzinga (Artifice, Beamsville), who created for Christmas one year at my request, the metal work on the back of my garage, which is depicted in the back cover photo of this book. 'Have I Told You Lately That I Love You?' is the musical theme of the piece – a song that Rick and I claimed as our own.

Thank you Frank and Frieda Storen, my parents. I also had too short a time with both of you; you have been gone twenty seven years. Thank you Dad for my love of words and thank you dear Mum (a.k.a Frieda Babes) for my love of music.

John Richard McBay – you said I should write and that I had a book in me somewhere. It turns out it was about us.

Thank you, here it is and I love you.

My God, Creator and protector who is writing a masterpiece as He puts me, this lovely mess back together again.

References

Tim Yearington, *That Native Thing, Exploring the Medicine Wheel* (2010, Borealis Press Ltd.)

Michael Wittmer, *Heaven Is A Place On Earth* (2004, Zondervan)

Joan Didion, *The Year of Magical Thinking* (2006 Vintage Books)

Jerry Sittser, *A Grace Disguised* (2004, Zondervan)

The Bible, (Revised Standard Version) (2002, Zondervan)

Macan Delavan, *Songs of Faith and Praise* (1992, Integrity Music, Inc.)

Lanny Wolfe, (1977, Lanny Wolfe Music/ASCAP)

Dr. David Kuhl, M.D., *What Dying People Want, Practical Wisdom for the End of Life* (2003, Anchor Canada)

Pam Belluck, *Families May Gain From Observing CPR* (March 13, 2013, New York Times)

George Matheson, *O Love That Will Not Let Me Go* (1842) Songs of Faith and Praise (1997, Howard Publishing)

John Thomas McFarland, *Away In a Manger* (1892) Songs of Faith and Praise (1997, Howard Publishing)

About the Author

First time author Sandra (Sandy) Elizabeth McBay pays homage with this book to Rick, her husband of 35.5 years and the hundreds of people she has walked beside in palliative care and bereavement support. After the death of her parents in 1988, Sandy pursued palliative, contemplative end of life and bereavement education to satisfy the innate desire to help others with the most important final task of life – death, and those left behind to find their way without their loved ones.

Sandy has been an educator of palliative visiting volunteers and a bereavement support facilitator for 25 years. She and her husband Rick had finally got to a place in their marriage where a deeper understanding of their lifetime commitment to each other was solidified and fun. When Rick died most suddenly and unexpectedly in 2010, Sandy's new reality and her love for words compelled her to write this book.

Sandy's sons Brian and Terral have also found professions of helping others, and they with their wives and 5 children continue to give her joy.

CPSIA information can be obtained
at www.ICGtesting.com
Printed in the USA
LVOW04s1956120116
470314LV00014B/376/P